THE ULTIMATE SHART SURVIVAL GUIDE

Gut Warnings, Clean-Up, Odor Control, Rebuilding Confidence, and Making a Clean Getaway!

JACK HAYNES

ISBN: 978-1-957590-51-6

For questions, email: Support@AwesomeReads.org

Please consider writing a review!

Just visit: AwesomeReads.org/review

FREE BONUS

SCAN TO GET OUR NEXT BOOK FOR FREE!

TABLE OF CONTENTS

INTRODUCTION

There are many embarrassing social faux pas that you can commit on a daily basis, like tripping over nothing, waving at someone who wasn't waving at you, mistaking a handshake for a hug, congratulating someone on being pregnant when they aren't, or walking into the wrong bathroom.

There is one that stands out above all the rest, with the soul-crushing humiliation that is second to none. It is so gut-wrenching that it will produce nightmares for years to come, trauma that will have to be unpacked with an unsuspecting therapist down the road, and anxiety that is second to none, all thanks to one bodily function.

Is it a natural body function, an avoidable habit, or just a surprise of the worst kind? What is this life-altering and mind-blowing event, you ask? The Shart. The bane of all ages, and the sort of thing no one wants to be remembered by. If you are one of the thirty-three percent of people that has experienced this, you are probably wondering how to handle it if it happens again.

Good news! In this book, we'll prepare you for the worst. This is the personal guide for anyone who is digestively doomed. Learn what this gross phenomenon is, and how to know when it might happen. You'll also learn what to do once the dreaded shart has come. There are a lot of steps to properly navigate this potential social landmine, and you don't want to miss a single one. Avoid the nasty odors and the exclamations of disgust with a careful plan.

When you've hit rock bottom and there is nowhere to go but up, make sure to read about how to rebuild your confidence and recover from the mental devastation that comes from sharting your pants. Learn to truly embrace yourself, even at your worst.

For those of you who haven't experienced this truly horrific event, learn how to avoid it and maybe stay out of the not-so-privileged group of sharters. Learn what foods can help, and what foods can hurt your sharting journey. There is no reason you should make it easy on your body to betray you with an unexpected shart.

Sometimes it is unavoidable, so know how to play it off without losing your cool, and how to shart proof your lifestyle. But no worries, it happens, and you'll get an opportunity to read about other people's mishaps and misery. You'll especially love this part if you have had an embarrassing shart story yourself because misery does love company. Fear not, you'll also learn how to see the humor in this social blunder. Because no matter how mortified you feel, you are not alone.

Before you are done with this book, that social blunder will turn from a fumble and a stumble into just another interesting part of what makes you the awesome person you are.

[1]
KNOW THY GUT: WARNING SIGNS & RISK FACTORS

One of the best ways that you can avoid the misapprehension of "will I?" or "won't I?" is to know your gut and be on the lookout for warning signs. With a little knowledge, you can understand the risk factors and keep yourself out of a flub of a situation. It doesn't take but a slight miscalculation on your part for a tragic incident to occur.

A cruel twist of digestive fate or a life-altering, pants-ruining, dignity-destroying event. The shart is better prepared for than left until the worst happens.

WHAT IS A SHART (AND WHY IT HAPPENS)

Perhaps you've heard of it, or maybe you've never encountered the term, but you've been worrying all this time about what the unfortunate thing that happened to you is. Sharting is when you pass gas (fart) and something unexpected comes out with the gas, leading to defecation (sh*tting). The two words combine to give the modern term: shart. Sharting can also be described as an unexpected and accidental expulsion of feces when internal gas escapes. Or, in medical terms, fecal incontinence.

The two origin words, fart and sh*t, tell quite a story themselves. The term sh*t comes from the Old English language, with the word scite meaning dung, scitte meaning diarrhea, and scitan meaning to defecate. These words came together to create schitte, and eventually morphed into the modern sh*t. While the word is considered a profanity in most of the world, the severity of the word varies depending on the culture in which it is used. Other words that also refer to excrement include poop, feces, dung, scat, stool, waste, and guano. The other root word, fart, referring to the passing of gas, is one of the oldest words in the English language, and hails from several words in Greek and Latin. Some other terms are cutting the cheese, breaking wind, gas, toot, letting one slip, flatulency, and poot.

While the term shart was being used in the early 2000s, it wasn't until the movie Along Came Polly that the term really gained popularity. Over the years, the term has attained its place in pop culture and has become an official term. It can be heard in classrooms across America, in restaurants, clubs, doctors' offices, and even the occasional professional setting. How do you know that you might be on the cusp of this disaster? Read on for early warning signs.

RECOGNIZING THE EARLY WARNING SIGNS OF A DISASTER

If you find yourself with an excessive amount of gas, it is time to get alert and be aware. Once gas builds up in the body, you may notice an increase in gas, abdominal cramps, stomach bloating, or a noticeable increase in your stomach size.

While some burping is normal, especially after eating or drinking something carbonated, excessive burping can indicate that there is gas in the pipes. While the average person can pass gas up to twenty times a day, more burping is an indication that more toots are on the way. There is no way to avoid all gas because it is part of the digestive system.

While farting can be embarrassing, especially if you pass the dreaded silent but deadly gas, it rarely leads to emergency situations. So, what takes a mostly innocent fart into the nightmare realm of sharting, and how do you tell the difference? If, when you toot, you notice a wet feeling or bubbling sensation, then you have crossed over into "uh-oh" territory.

If you notice that you have gas and your stomach is giving suspicious rumblings, it is best to head to a bathroom as quickly as possible and let your body do what it is built to do.

THE GUT CONNECTIONS: HOW THE DIGESTIVE SYSTEM WORKS

Gas and poop are the byproducts of your digestive system, and understanding how it works can help you know what is happening inside your body. The digestive system is your body's food processor and is essential to keeping your body happy and healthy. But it does create poop and gas.

Your digestive system is at work before you take your first bite of food. It starts with the saliva in your mouth, which begins to produce more when you smell something delicious or see something appetizing. Your body can make one to two liters of saliva daily. When you start eating, the saliva helps break down the food in your mouth into something that your tongue can push down your throat. The spit, teeth, and tongue all work together to make your food into a mushy state that can be sent into the second part of your digestive tract, the esophagus.

The esophagus is a ten-inch-long, stretchy tube that carries food from your mouth, where it has been ground down, to your stomach on a journey that takes about five to eight seconds. The muscles in the esophagus are so strong that if you had to, you could eat upside down, and the food would still travel to the stomach. The wavelike motion of the muscles moving food through your esophagus is called peristalsis.

Once the food reaches your stomach, it is mixed with the acids that your stomach carries. The stomach acid helps break down the food even further, and the muscles in your stomach help accelerate the process. The stomach is also where food is stored until it is ready to move on to the next stage. The thick liquid in your stomach that food becomes when partially digested and mixed with gastric juices is called chyme. One of the important jobs of your stomach acid is to kill bacteria that might creep into your body. Your stomach replaces its lining every three to four days because of the strength of the acid in your stomach, which would burn your skin. Food stays in your stomach for three to four hours.

Once your stomach has finished digesting the food, it passes it along to the small intestine. The small intestine is so compacted in your body that if you stretched it out, it would be over twenty-two feet long and is called small only because it is one inch wide. As the food passes through the small intestine, the nutrients are absorbed and delivered to other parts of your body.

After spending up to six hours in the small intestine, food makes its way to the large intestine. Once there, the rest of the liquid and minerals are removed, leaving the poop. It can take up to three days for the large intestine to complete the processing of your food, after which it is passed to the anus. The anus or butt is where food is expelled from the body about once a day.

Now, what about that process causes gas? Sometimes, when eating, you can accidentally swallow air, which then passes through your body. However, stomach gases are the main culprit of gas, as excess air is created when certain foods are broken down.

RISKY FOODS
THAT TEMPT FATE

While we all want to eat what we enjoy, certain foods create more gas in the digestive process. It might be a good idea to avoid some of these foods when you are going to be in an enclosed space or around other people, where a shart would be quickly noticed and highly embarrassing.

Veggies can turn on you. Especially high fiber vegetables that contain carbs, fiber, and sulfur compounds. One of the largest villains in the story of the dangerous vegetable is broccoli, which contains a compound called raffinose, along with sulfur. Eating raw broccoli, while healthy in many ways, is an almost guaranteed way to get yourself some extra gas. Instead of eating it raw, try steaming it to soften some of those fibers.

Another vegetable threat is Brussels sprouts. Avoid eating Brussels sprouts that have been fried or cooked in oil because they can cause even more gas buildup and production. Try parboiling and then roasting them, making it a less gassy treat. Avoid other vegetables like cauliflower, spinach, asparagus, and onions.

Some fruits can also cause gas, which might lead to an unexpected shart because of the high levels of fructose, sorbitol, and fiber in them. Apples, while they might keep the doctor away, can also keep your friend away if you are eating large amounts of them. The excellent fruit is a good source of fiber, vitamin C, and antioxidants, but eating them raw or juiced can increase your toot timing. Try baking apples to break down some of the sugar alcohol and the fiber. While it might take a lot of work to eat enough to cause problems, cherries can also be a gassy offender. If you need your cherry fix, consider cooked cherries to help reduce the windiness in your trousers.

At least sixty-five percent of the world's population is to some degree lactose intolerant, so don't be surprised to find yourself particularly flatulent after eating dairy. Milk is the top suspect when it comes to gas-producing dairy products. Avoid milk and try to replace it with lactose-free milk or even milk alternatives. There are some great almond or soy milks if you are concerned about public disgrace. Cheese, the love of many, has also been known to cause gastric upsets. If you are a cheesehead, don't despair; some cheeses have lower levels of lactose, such as Parmesan, Cheddar, Swiss, Gouda, and Provolone. It is best to avoid fresh, creamy cheese, as it can cause you to visit the bathroom. Probably the most heartbreaking thing for lactose-intolerant people everywhere is ice cream. Try a dairy-free ice cream or stick to sorbet.

BEVERAGES THAT ARE BOUND TO BACKFIRE

It can't be a big surprise to realize that sodas can have a lot of gas buildup, since they bubble so much themselves. Carbonation from the drink adds air to your body. A special warning note to diet sodas, which contain artificial sweeteners, is that they are a massive contributor to your body's gassiness. If you find yourself craving your favorite soda, avoid chugging it cold and instead open it, allowing the gases to escape before drinking it slowly.

Beer, another drink of the people, is also a gas contributor. Carbonation and fermentation lead to excess gas and unnecessary bloating. Especially when paired with greasy food, which slows down digestion and gives the beer more time to produce gas. If you want to enjoy a cold one, try to pair it with a protein-rich meal while savoring your drink.

Perhaps unexpectedly, there are certain types of water that produce significant amounts of gas. Maybe slightly less unexpected is the fact that the gassy water is sparkling water. Much like soda, the carbonation of the sparkling water can lead to troublesome tummy times. Let your bubbly sit after being opened to release a good bit of the excess air that will lead to possible sharting incidents.

Smoothies can be something to avoid in certain situations, as well. Because of the fresh fruit and vegetables, smoothies are ripe for rumbling rumination. If you want to enjoy the health benefits of smoothies, try to drink them on days you'll be home and around a bathroom.

TRAVEL SHARTS: WHY AIRPLANES & ROAD TRIPS ARE DANGEROUS

If you won't be at home, being aware of what you eat is important. A worst-case scenario is being trapped on a plane, train, or other confined space with innocent bystanders. The last thing you want to do is be accused of eco-terrorism after crop dusting a group of fellow travelers with noxious fumes.

When you are on an airplane, there are limited bathroom spaces, which means that you might not be able to get to one in time. There is no hiding a shart when you are sitting inches away from your neighbor, and they will quickly be able to hunt down the source of the smell. It will be impossible for you to hide your actions if you have to squeeze in front of the person in the aisle seat with a wonderful brown stain decorating your derriere.

Another worst-case scenario is when you are going on an extended road trip. There is nothing better than piling into your car with friends or family, heading to a wildly anticipated destination, or taking a meandering route, with snacks to sustain you on your journey. When, unexpectedly, your tummy starts rumbling and you try to ignore it. Maybe the rumbling gets worse, so you convince your fellow riders to let down the windows and enjoy the fresh air. Suddenly, the gas you expect to exit your body brings along a visitor. Best-case scenario, you just stink the rest of the trip. But worst-case scenario, you leave a stain behind on the upholstery for everyone to stare at the rest of the journey.

When traveling, it is the perfect time to stay extra diligent about what you are eating. Before you set out on your trip, visit a private restroom and do all your business beforehand. An empty bowel is less likely to lead to an embarrassing trip.

TIMES YOU'RE MOST AT RISK

Other places are touch-and-go for a person with gas. It doesn't just have to be while you are traveling. It can also happen when you are hanging out at your local haunts or going to a special occasion right in your local town.

You could be at your gym in the middle of a deadlift when you are straining to come up. You don't realize that what you thought was pressure from the heavyweight is actually a fart working its way out with lots of juicy company. There is no little puff from you, but more of a flood of regret. There is no walk to the locker room that doesn't involve a waddle.

Maybe you are at the mall trying on a new pair of pants. They look amazing; they are the perfect pair of jeans. Then your stomach suddenly starts cramping, and deep breaths lead you to releasing what you assume is just a massive buildup of gas, but air isn't the only thing that comes out. Now you get to buy your perfect pair of jeans just to get out of the store and avoid eye contact while you scurry out.

You've been waiting for a callback from your dream job and have finally landed an interview. Wearing your best business outfit and a winning smile, you head into the interview. While describing all the amazing experiences you have and how wonderful you would be for the role, you excitedly move around, only to realize that you've let loose something unexpected. Once the interviewer starts sniffing, you know there is no way to finish with dignity, and no amount of professional smiling will keep them from immediately telling this story around the water cooler. Nothing left to do but get up and make the final walk of shame before starting job hunting all over.

Maybe it's your first date, or maybe it is one of many you've had. This person could be the love of your life, your future partner, and your beloved co-parent if the dates keep going well. Unfortunately, you had a smoothie with extra yogurt in it for breakfast, and now your stomach is letting you know its displeasure. You can't walk away while your date is in the middle of telling you about their parents, and the sweat is breaking out on your upper lip. You think you'll just let one slip out quietly and gently. But that is not what happens. Cutting a date short mid-story is a great way to not get another date. But you don't have a choice and just hope they don't realize you are walking funny as you leave.

Being aware of your body and what is happening is a great way to avoid some of these scenarios. But that doesn't mean that you won't shart unexpectedly.

YOUR GUT'S BETRAYAL TIMELINE: FROM RUMBLE TO RUIN

What kind of buildup can you expect before a traumatizing moment befalls you? There is no set timeline, but it might seem a little like this:

You have a wonderful meal and proceed to have a wonderful day. It is the kind of day that makes you want to skip down the street. It never occurs to you that the burger or pasta you had for lunch might be about to come back with a vengeance.

Unexpectedly, you find that you have to burp. Just a little one that no one notices, and you don't think much about the small gas escape. Next, you find that your stomach is rumbling and gurgling, but it is so light that you aren't even sure if it is real or your imagination. Without thinking much about it, you go on with your wonderful day, until suddenly there it is again: a rumble.

You realize that there is a slight buildup of pressure in your stomach and that it is getting worse. In an effort to release some of the pressure and stop the cramping, you let a little toot lose and instantly feel better. You are ready to continue with your day.

Soon after, you realize the pressure is back and building faster than before. You try to ignore it and convince yourself that you can hold it, but deep breathing and muscle clenching will only get you so far with that kind of pressure. There isn't anywhere to go to the restroom, so you just pick a quiet corner and discreetly let out another little toot. This time, more gas comes flooding out, and you realize that the gas wasn't alone. Warmth floods your rear regions, followed by realization, and then regret. That regret is quickly followed by the smell.

While this might not have happened to you yet, don't fool yourself into believing that it can't. It is best to be prepared and ready for the unexpected. You don't have to be a Boy Scout to have all the tools you need in the worst-case shart scenario.

[2]
CRISIS RESPONSE:
THE CLEANUP PROTOCOL

Once the worst has happened, and you find yourself in a compromising position with a heavy load in the back, it is time to start planning what you are going to do next. These next few moments will determine precisely how legendary your body's betrayal is going to be. If you are smart, quick, and lucky, you might get away with minimal damage and a spot of dignity.

THE "OH NO" MOMENT: WHAT TO DO FIRST

While it might seem counterintuitive, the first thing you need to do after a blowout is to freeze. Assess the damage. Take note of where and how many people are around you. If they haven't noticed, it is crucial to keep them unaware of your troublesome situation. Try to figure out exactly what is happening in your drawers. Is it small and contained, or do you have a slurpy running down your legs?

Shift slightly to check the squish factor. You need to know if you're dealing with a minor leak or a full-blown lava flow; vital information to have if you need to make a next step plan. Make sure you are in control of your face. Nothing gives away an uncomfortable situation faster than having on your "oh no" face (tight lips, wide eyes, and the subtle aura of inner screaming). Look calm, cool, and collected, even if you are panicking on the inside. Don't avoid eye contact. Just smile and nod like nothing life-altering is happening. With the right attitude, you might get out of the situation with your pride still intact.

Be aware of your surroundings. Is there somewhere you can stealthily move away from other people, or a dark corner you can go to hide? Once you are in a secure location that requires minimal movement, perform a sniff check. You don't want to, no one wants to, but you have to know how bad the damage is. Do you smell like a rotten sewage drain left in the sun? Or maybe just a mild manure-gone-bad-odor? The severity of the smell will determine just how much space you need to give people around you.

Once you understand the severity of the situation, it is time to plan an escape route. The first step is to determine if you need to make any excuses before leaving. For mild smells, you can calmly extricate yourself from the situation, but if the odor is a ten out of ten—run. Apologizing is easier than trying to explain.

If you have to sit down at any point, make sure you protect the seat. DO NOT leave evidence behind when you finally escape to find your decorum. Props are your friend right now. If you have a jacket, take it off and wrap it around your waist. Better people think you have no fashion sense than realize the truth. Would you prefer to be remembered as the person who did something weird with their jacket or the person who pooped in their pants and poisoned the air?

Backpack, computer case, purse, or small child; if you are creative, most things can be used to cover your shame.

CLEANING UP
WITH DIGNITY

When you have finally found a place to try to pull yourself together, take a moment and breathe, assuming the smell isn't so bad you can't. Just remember, you aren't the first human, and won't be the last, to go through this embarrassing situation. The anxiety attack and self-hate spiral can come later. Right now, it's time to clean up. Channel your favorite action character and imagine that you are handling this situation with the precision of a bomb technician.

Now the name of the game is survival and sanitation. Approach your bathroom like nothing is wrong and make sure there's a lock. What is worse than sharting yourself? Having someone walk in while you attempt to clean yourself up. Locked in your sanctuary, it is time to remove the affected clothing. This will be your first, true look at just how bad the accident has become.

With all the affected layers removed, assess just how much damage has been done. The material and clothing you wear will make a big difference in what you need to do.

If you are wearing cotton, know that the stain will spread fast and go far because of the absorbency rate of cotton. If you are wearing dark cotton, you might be in luck and manage to keep this shameful secret while you rush home.

If you are wearing polyester, you might be in luck because it will help contain the spillage, but you might as well throw that away when you get home. Polyester is notorious for holding smells that aren't a smell you want to carry with you.

Wool is not going to be the best-case scenario. It will quickly absorb smells and liquids. It will be a lot of trouble to clean, and it probably won't help contain the smell at all. Wool is a natural material and might be dry-clean-only. Sometimes it is less embarrassing to let go of your favorite pair of work pants than to explain the stain on them.

Denim is thick enough that it might help keep the mess inside, and the good news is that it is easy to wash. Once you make it home, there is a good chance that you can run your denim through the washer on a deep clean and come out of the other side alright.

No matter what material you are wearing, there are limited options in the bathroom; if you are unprepared for the situation you find yourself in. Once you have assessed the damage, it is time to start trying to salvage the situation.

Get yourself cleaned up first. If you are in a stall, use toilet paper to clean yourself up first. Ideally, you are in a bathroom with access to a sink, where you can clean up with towels and soap, but if a stall is all you have to work with, then you'll have to make the most of the toilet paper.

If you have any extra layers, go ahead and put them in the disposal pile. You aren't trying to walk out of there with your cotton undies, just some dignity. The more you can dispose of, the less you have to clean, and the less smell you carry with you on the way out and home.

Start with the least affected areas and work up to the main event when cleaning your clothes. Get as much as possible with toilet paper. If you have access to the sink, go ahead and run your clothes under cold water. Hot water is going to bake in the stain and smell. Always run the water from the backside so you don't push the stain farther into the material. When the situation is dire enough, go ahead and use some hand soap to help with the cleanup.

Check if the bathroom has some air fresheners. Go ahead and apply some to your clothes. Better to smell like original citrus or lavender fields than Eau de Poop. Once you have done everything you can, it is time to figure out how to buy new clothes or take yourself home.

WHAT IF THERE'S
NO TOILET PAPER?

When you walk into the bathroom and think you are finally in the home stretch to a solution, sometimes the worst happens, and you realize that you have no toilet paper. If it is just the stall, wait until another one opens up and pop on over. But rarely is the solution that simple. With your luck, the entire bathroom has none.

Look for toilet seat covers. A lot of restrooms have them in a dispenser on the wall behind the commode. It is one of the first things you should check anytime you go into a restroom, and it will work as a thinner, less effective type of paper.

If there aren't any covers, head to the sink and see if they at least managed to restock the paper towels. While they might be scratchy and less ideal than your preferred four-ply, at least they'll get the job done. Tear them up into the needed sizes and get to work.

There are no covers and no paper towels. It looks like no one has stocked this bathroom since flip phones were popular. The good news is that there are probably still toilet paper rolls in the stall. Unroll those little cardboard lifesavers and get to work.

Before you resort to some of the more dramatic options, check your pockets, purse, work bag, and anywhere else you might have something stuffed. Old napkins, receipt paper, notes, or a leftover face mask can all do the job in this improvised situation. Being creative and flexible is your only hope.

BAG, BIN, FLUSH, OR BURN: WHAT TO DO WITH YOUR UNDIES

The first step in deciding what to do with your incriminating evidence is to determine how bad the situation is. Are you looking at a mild staining that could be handled with some Oxiclean, a moderate overflow that a good soaking could fix, or a catastrophe that you and God both know those undies won't come back from?

Also, consider the value of the underwear in question. If you grabbed them for two dollars at the bargain bin, it is probably a good idea to just let them go. They've done their job and are ready for retirement. Once you have determined that the underwear can be released, you need to decide what to do with them. As classy as it is to leave your drawers on the floor of the bathroom, there are better options.

If you have access to a plastic bag, a shopping bag, or another material that blocks odors, that should be your first choice. Unfortunately, you might not be carrying what you need to discreetly tuck the smell bomb away, and you can turn to paper. Use toilet paper or paper towels to wrap your poopy package up neatly. Then stick it into the bathroom trash can, making sure to push it past the top layer to hide the sight and smell of your shame.

Don't try flushing your underwear. It might seem like an elegant solution, but you will quickly change your mind once the toilet starts backing up and the neighboring stalls start screaming about toilet water running over their nice shoes.

CARING FOR YOUR CLOTHING CASUALTIES

Once you've made it home, you still aren't done handling your crisis. Most of the time, you'll be bringing your evidence home with you, either in the clothes you are wearing or in a tightly sealed bag. Getting them in the wash and looking brand new is the goal now.

Look at some different options at your local store. The laundry aisle will have a rainbow of plastic bottles, all claiming to be the solution to every problem you have. Some that will work better, and some you might as well leave behind on the shelf. Here's what to look for:

Enzyme-based detergents work to break down organic and protein-based stains. These will work for what you are trying to do. Look for brands like Biokleen enzyme detergent or Dirty Labs enzyme detergent.

Stain removers and pretreat sprays are another go-to option. If you already have a detergent you like, try pretreating to make sure the stain and odor come out. OxiClean is one of the go-to stain treatments available.

If neither of those options works for you, try adding more odor-neutralizing options. These won't target the stain, but they'll make sure you don't have a flashback every time you smell your pants. Lysol Sanitizer, Pine-Sol, and Odoban Laundry are options that will fix your smells up right away.

If you don't like the idea of turning to chemicals to solve your problems, there are a lot of natural options out there as well. These will help you tackle stains and remove odors as well as any supermarket find.

Baking soda is the workhorse of cleaning. It will neutralize odors and combat stains. Adding a scoop of baking soda to your wash is always a good idea, and it's available for purchase in bulk.

White vinegar is often considered a go-to cleaner and laundry detergent for many people. It will kill any smells that are hanging around your drawers by destroying the bacteria that cause them. Just a half cup in each load of laundry can make a huge difference.

Don't ever forget that hydrogen peroxide can remove odors and whiten your laundry without bleaching. There aren't too many stains that hydrogen peroxide won't fix right up. It can also be used for everything from a bathroom cleaner to a teeth-whitening mouthwash.

THE UH-OH
PORTABLE FIVE-STEP GUIDE

STEP ONE: STAY CALM

- Freeze. Assess the squish.
- Control your face. You're an actor now.
- Look for exits, shadows, and cover.

STEP TWO: MOVE SMART

- Power walk to safety, not an Olympic sprint.
- Avoid crowded bathrooms if possible.
- Find the "Golden Stall" (clean, isolated, quiet).

STEP THREE: WIPE, WASH, WIN

- Undies? Assess damage.
- Use toilet paper, seat covers, or napkins.
- Soap + cold water = best combo.

STEP FOUR: DISPOSE OF THE EVIDENCE

- Wrap in paper. Bury it in the trash can.
- NEVER flush underwear. It's not worth it.
- Bonus: double bag if possible.

STEP FIVE: EXIT STRATEGY

- Hoodie around the waist.
- Bag, laptop, small child-use what you've got.
- Don't explain. Just walk with purpose.

[3]
SURVIVING
PUBLIC RESTROOMS

PUBLIC RESTROOM SURVIVAL TECHNIQUES

If your concerns are high about shartings, farts, and all things gastrointestinal, then you might be spending a lot of time in restrooms. Here are some basic guidelines for both public and private restrooms to make sure you are not leaving a bad impression. You'd hate to leave someone thinking you are the villain of the bathroom story.

Keep your socializing to a minimum when you are in a stall. No one wants to hear your life story or how your day is going while trying to relieve themselves. Save the small talk for your coffee shop and respect the code of silence in the bathroom.

Flush. There shouldn't be a lot to explain about this common courtesy. No matter where you have found to give your bladder some relief, have the decency to flush when you are done. One or two flushes make sure it goes down the drain. If you have to wait and flush a second time, take the time to get the job done right. There is nothing worse than walking into a bathroom and seeing the remnants of someone's burrito.

Hover if you want. Some people don't want to make contact with the germ-infested toilet seat, and that is understandable. If you spend enough time on leg day to handle the hover, it is a great way to avoid the seat, but make sure you clean up after any splashing or missing. Don't leave the seat dirtier than you found it.

Wash your hands when you are ready to leave the bathroom. Don't take potty germs out into the world. Maybe when you were a child, you were told, or you have heard a child told, to sing the birthday song twice. That rule still applies. You didn't magically get stronger than the germs and need less handwashing time. While, as an adult, you have many appointments to keep and places to be, it's best to do it with clean hands.

If you clog, own it. Don't do the damage and then try to sneak out. Let the appropriate person know, especially if you are at a private residence. Your best hope is to find a plunger nearby and handle the bubbling cauldron yourself without alerting anyone. But if no plunger is available, quietly hunt the host down and request one. A good host won't ask any questions and will just give you what you need to handle the situation. If you are in a public restroom, it isn't always so easy to find a solution. Make an effort to check any nearby utility closets for a plunger. If there isn't one, let an employee know. You don't have to fess up to the mess. Just let them know you are making them aware of the situation.

When it comes to the bathroom, leave no proof you were ever there. Be considerate of your fellow bathroomers, both present and future.

Now that you are a bathroom expert and emergency situation pro, here is a helpful checklist to keep with you so you don't panic.

EMERGENCY BATHROOM TACTICS: FASTEST ROUTES & STALL SELECTION

Once you have made your escape, it is time to head straight to the closest bathroom. Move fast but be smart. Being aware of the surrounding bathrooms is always a good idea. When you go to a new space, scope out the lay of the land. There is no reason to go unprepared, and sharting isn't the only disaster that can happen. From spilling food on yourself to escaping unpleasant conversations, bathrooms are always the answer.

If you are a pro, you'll know where that one bathroom is. You know the one. It is a little farther away, a little more isolated, a little cleaner, and a little quieter. It is the bathroom that no one talks about because you all collectively want to keep the bathroom defilers away from your safe spot. Never mind that you are about to become a bathroom defiler yourself.

When you move to the bathroom, make sure to move at a normal speed. Nothing will scream "panic problems" and attract attention faster than you making a Hail Mary sprint for the bathroom. Think power walking to a meeting, not "holy moly I've got a pants problem" speed.

When you get to the restroom, take a minute to listen. If you hear voices inside, keep moving. You need a bathroom fast, but you need privacy more because there is no hiding the smell leaking from your backside once you are in a bathroom. If you can find a family-style bathroom or another type of bathroom with one stall, that is the perfect place. If there is no suitable bathroom, consider the building you are in. Is there an upstairs? Maybe somewhere next door? Don't be scared to think outside the box to come up with a better solution.

If you have had a level five blowout and are leaking, distance becomes the enemy, and you'll just have to head to the closest bathroom and throw what remains of your good name to the wind. There is no hiding a trail leading directly to you. As a kindness to yourself, avoid mirrors. There is no reason to see what is going on until you are in the bathroom and can do something about it.

TACTICAL USE OF PAPER TOWELS, SOCKS, & FAST-FOOD NAPKINS

While paper towels can be overlooked in many situations, they are gold in disposable form. Keep a roll in your car or a bag you keep with you. Don't ever be caught far from home, or just down the street, without them. They are durable, absorbent, and disposable. Great for wiping down unfortunate areas, wrapping up things better left out of the light of day, or offering some padding to disaster zones.

If you have assessed your situation and come to the conclusion that you are well and truly screwed without any supplies or emergency preparedness, take a look at your shoes. There is a chance that the innocent sock that has been soaking up your foot sweat might be about to save your behind, or rather save you from what came out of your behind. A cotton sock will work in a pinch, which is something many people overlook, but necessity is the mother of invention.

Another last-ditch effort is to dig around for fast-food napkins. Maybe on your quick escape to the restroom, you pass a kitchen, gathering area, or hangout room. Stop and check the drawers. Most of the time, no one wants to throw away unused napkins from restaurants and will collect them in common places. Don't be afraid to look.

Note that none of these materials can be flushed; they must be disposed of in the trash. Keep in mind that these last-minute heroes can also be used in different combinations to meet the needs of your situation.

CLEANING SUPPLIES TO KEEP ON YOU (OR IN YOUR CAR)

You've envisioned all the worst-case scenarios where you are stranded and embarrassed at the mercy of whatever local bathroom you can find, but let's imagine a scenario where you are actually prepared. Having the right supplies on hand or nearby can change the game and make sure you don't become the butt of office jokes or the punchline your friends can't wait to crack.

THE HYGIENE KIT TO GIVE YOUR DIGNITY A FIGHTING CHANCE

FLUSHABLE WIPES

While toilet paper can get the job done, sometimes it leaves your tush more raw than comfortable. A flushable wipe will remove the evidence much cleaner and faster than dry toilet paper. Even if you don't have a bathroom emergency, it can be a good idea to keep a travel pack in your purse, backpack, or briefcase. Lots of different brands are available, and your future self will thank you for being prepared.

SEALABLE PLASTIC BAGS

In emergency situations, having a way to dispose of evidence is important. You never know when you might commit a toilet crime or some other nefarious crime that needs prompt evidence disposal. Having sandwich-sized and gallon-sized bags will allow you to put undies, pants, or other contaminated pieces into a smell-proof hidey hole. If the situation is extremely dire, channel your inner crime scene cleanup crew, and double-bag that bad boy.

EXTRA UNDERWEAR

Go ahead and put your Ziploc bag to use by keeping an extra pair of underwear tucked in there. It will keep them clean and make sure you have a backup pair. Sharting is not the only reason to keep spare panties. You might need another pair for an innocent reason, like walking outside on a hot day and sweating through your first pair.

TRAVEL-SIZED BOTTLE OF HAND SANITIZER

Really, this one ought to be self-evident. If you are going through your day-to-day life without hand sanitizer, stop it immediately. The world is a nasty place. Stop walking through it, collecting germs like they are your favorite Pokémon. Hand sanitizer is good to use anytime you are in public spaces and touch things, especially when you are in a public restroom, because what if, heaven forbid, there is no soap. And if you are a person who doesn't wash their hands at all in the bathroom . . . you might as well stop reading now. You are going to need a lot more help than this book can provide.

DEODEORIZING SPRAY OR BODY MIST

Having something that can help correct your personal hazardous atmosphere is vital when you've had a juicy fart. No one will believe that nothing happened if you walk around smelling like the local sewage grate. Either spray can help you conceal the smell in the room and on yourself. Look for smaller, travel-size bottles if you want to be discreet.

PLASTIC GLOVES

Plastic gloves are pretty self-explanatory; unless you've got a weird fetish, there is nothing in that cleanup situation that you want on your hands. Save yourself the agony and have plastic gloves to put on, which will help keep your hands clean and stink-free.

DISINFECTING SPRAY

If you have ever worked a job that required you to clean public restrooms, you'll be very familiar with how nasty public restrooms are. The public has no decency and can leave a bathroom unfit for animals. Even in private restrooms, there is no guarantee of how well the cleaners have done, so if it brings you peace of mind, give everything a good misting before getting down to business.

BONUS POINTS

Extra clothes (from extreme uh-ohs), small trash bags (for more evidence concealing options), and a compact mirror (to really check what's going on in the back).

Keeping these items on hand doesn't prevent an accident from happening, but they make sure that you are as prepared as possible to deal with any fallout . . . or the things that fallout.

STRATEGIC SEATING: ALWAYS HAVE AN ESCAPE ROUTE

When you think there might be an upcoming disaster, maybe because you've eaten disagreeable foods or your stomach has been particularly upset, plan your seating.

One of the most dreaded accidents is the cinema shart. There is nothing worse than realizing that you have a heavy load in the back and you now have to squeeze in front of several people's faces as you make your walk of shame out of the row. Avoid that by sitting on the end. No reason to miss your movie. Just be prepared for a quick exit.

If you are going out to eat, just explain to your fellow diners that you are claustrophobic and need the end seat. Most people won't argue with you. If you do find yourself in a standoff about an easy-to-escape seat, perhaps the other person is having a similar stomach rebellion day. Compromise by finding a table with no booths, and all chairs that are easy to escape.

When choosing your seat, avoid sitting directly in front of an air vent. The last thing you need is the squishy mess getting wafted around the room even faster. There is nothing worse than the smell of a rotting outhouse traveling at air-conditioning speed. Trust me, once it hits the fan (literally), you're no longer just dealing with a shart—you're dealing with a crime scene.

LOUD MUSIC, HAND DRYERS, & OTHER AUDIO CAMOUFLAGE

When you find your body ready to realize a plume of despair, the fart, try to time it with other sounds. There is no denying what happens if a fart rips out in a quiet room, but if there are other sounds, you might be able to pull off the crime of the century.

If you find yourself in a crowded bathroom with no private relief available, consider turning on the hand dryers. That background noise will make it harder for anyone to hear, or maybe easier for everyone to ignore. Either way, it will be appreciated that you tried to mask the gag-worthy sound.

Don't forget that you can flush the toilet if you need a little sound coverage in the bathroom. You'll have to endure the splash of a flushing toilet, but there are worse things. Think of it as an unhygienic bidet.

You might get lucky in the bathroom and find a squeaky door. That would be ideal. No one will think twice about you messing with the door, trying to fix the squeaking, while you are actually giving your stomach the sweet relief it needs.

If you are somewhere with loud music playing, you are in luck. You've hit the gas relief jackpot. Make sure you don't wait until the end of a song because the encore everybody wants is not coming from your butt. Be prepared to move once you have let loose, especially if it is a heavy load. The smell might give you away.

If you find yourself in a quiet room, use what you have. Cough some to mask any sounds escaping your trousers, and maybe move your chair around. Between the scraping chair and hacking coughs, no one will hear you let loose some toots. And if something extra comes out, just be prepared to exit the room.

[4]
ODOR CONTROL &
DAMAGE MANAGEMENT

You've learned a lot about how to handle the physical evidence of an accidental shart, but that might not be the most dangerous part of an unexpected shart. While you can lean against a wall, tie something around yourself, scrub your pants, and use many other tricks to overcome the stain—how do you deal with the smell?

We have all been on the wrong end of a creeping fart stench. It slowly slithers its way along the floor and scales up the walls. Once the smell attaches to a nose, it is nearly impossible to get the cloying odor out. That rancid mist seems to linger for longer than any other bad smell, leaving you trapped in its stifling grip.

WHY IT SMELLS WORSE THAN DEATH

When we pass gas, the smell is so awful because of the mix of compounds in the gas. They are called volatile organic compounds (VOCs), also known as stinky gas.

That classic rotten egg stink? You can thank the bacteria in your gut for pumping out sulfur. The main source of the rotten egg smell often comes from bacteria in the large intestine that produces sulfur. It can also come from some foods or just the biology of your unique body.

Next up: methanethiol. It smells like cabbage that lost its will to live. It couldn't be fresh, healthy cabbage. Nope, methanethiol smells like rotting cabbage. Certain foods, especially cabbage, cause the body to produce methanethiol, which is released as gas.

Then there's skatole: the VIP of poop smells, which is produced by breaking down amino acids from protein-rich foods. It is most commonly referred to as the poop smell. It is what creates the actual smell that leads to people saying, "That smells like crap."

With that microbial mayhem going on in your gut, it is no wonder that your toots smell awful and can clear a room. Just farting is bad enough. But a shart? That's when the real stink symphony begins — hot, humid, and highly regrettable.

VOCs, like what makes up your farts, tend to become more effective at being smelly when heat and humidity are added. This means VOCs really shine in shart situations, where they are often hot and humid.

The higher the temperature, the faster the smell diffuses through an area. Higher temperatures mean more kinetic energy, increasing their speed through the air. Because sharts involve fecal substrates, the heat is higher, which leads to an even faster diffusion of smells.

Once the smells are released, the humidity causes the odor to transfer and cling to fabrics and other surfaces. The higher moisture also makes the smell easier to detect because your nose works best when damp, so humid air actually helps your nose pick up faint olfactory cues more easily.

Damp fabric binds odor molecules more tenaciously than dry materials. When your sweat or residue dampens underwear or pants, the moist environment lengthens how long VOCs hang out. Getting out of wet, stinky pants allows the smell to disperse and get away from you faster. It isn't your butt that is holding on to the smell; it is your pants.

TRAVEL-SIZED DEODORIZERS YOU SHOULD NEVER LEAVE HOME WITHOUT

You know you should have something to help cover smells because smells linger longer than stains, and can follow you around, leaving a cloud of despair. Save the noses of innocent bystanders and have a smell-good spray ready. But what works best?

Spray deodorants or body mists are a good option. When you are shopping for the right option, make sure that you look for an alcohol-based scent because it will evaporate quickly to help mask the stinky smells. Look for fresh smells like citrus or minty smells; they'll do a better job. Avoid heavy florals, or you'll smell like grandma's closet that had an unfortunate moment.

Fabric fresheners are another good option to have on hand because you can spray them directly on fabrics. Don't carry around a full-size bottle because they won't be discreet at all. Instead, look for travel-size bottles. If you can't find a small bottle, get a mini reusable spray bottle and just pour some of your product in.

Essential oils are wonderful for masking smells as well. Lavender, tea tree, and peppermint are all naturally deodorizing. A few drops of essential oil can help mask scents without being overpowering. Plus, lavender is relaxing, and you might need some relaxing after sharting your pants.

There are a lot of places you can keep your secret smell correction, including a glove box, laptop case, your shart kit, or any other place that is easily accessible in emergencies.

For the love of all that is holy, do not get a smell-good spray with glitter. While glitter is wonderful in a lot of situations, you do not want to leave glitter behind after you've just had an accident. No need to turn your shame into a disco ball.

HOMEMADE ODOR FIXES

If you find yourself drowning in the smell of regret without a body spray in sight, there are other options to consider, like trying dryer sheets. They have great smells that can mask bad smells, and it would be better to smell like "April fresh" than "May tragedy." You can rub them across fabric, or shove one down your pants.

Coffee grounds are an unexpected savior of the smelly. Their porous structure, which traps odor-causing molecules, and the high amount of nitrogen, which neutralizes smells, can be a more natural odor solution. Beware of coffee staining clothes, but it can be rubbed on darker clothing and skin before being brushed off. Keep a satchel of it in your car and other places for a coffee smell.

Dry shampoo might be a lifesaver for you if you don't have any traditional smell-good options. Use it just like a fabric freshener, but then shake out the white powder, unless you are wearing white, in which case it won't show. Even if you are wearing white, don't leave so much on the fabric that you shed a mini powder storm as you walk.

Vodka can also be a smell-saving strategy. Spray down any affected clothing and smell like a sad bachelorette party, but at least not like poop. The vodka will kill the odor-causing bacteria and evaporate quickly. Just don't stand too close to any open flames while your butt is drying. Vodka is also good for killing odors in shoes, gym clothes, and other places where fabric holds your smelly shame.

LAYERING CLOTHING: A SMELL BARRIER STRATEGY

No matter when your life takes the unexpected shart turn, your clothing can and should be your first line of defense. Your detour disaster might strike mid-errand, mid-date, or mid-workout, so there is no telling what you'll be wearing, but do the best you can with what is available.

The time-honored and classic waist wrap is always a good go-to. If you have a jacket, flannel, hoodie, or cardigan, tie the arms around your waist. Make sure it is tight enough that your makeshift cover doesn't slide off or come undone. Avoid slick material like your favorite tracksuit.

If you feel like an "incident" might be coming up, go ahead and add an extra layer or two of undies. Those extra layers will give you a disposable layer for small accidents, and a way to slow down the mess in more severe accidents. For bonus points, throw on a pair of spanks or bike shorts over your undies for a tighter, contained fit. Just remember, if your stomach is rumbling, double up.

Anytime you can wear a longer top, it can help cover many sins. If no one can see your derriere, then no one can prove the nose hair singeing smell is coming from you. Just keep moving fast, and don't let that top swish around.

Dark colored pants are also a good way to hedge your bets if you are leaving the house on a less-than-auspicious day. Don't ignore the warning signs that your body is angrily sending out.

Layering can trap odor closer to your body, which might sound bad, but it's better than letting it waft freely for all your neighbors to enjoy. Fabrics like denim and thick cotton trap and hold smell to your body better than synthetics that "breathe."

HOW TO KEEP THE STINK CONTAINED IN YOUR CAR

There is nothing worse than having a bad smell sink into your car. Every time you get in, you are reminded of your mortifying accident and how you meant to let a little gas slip, and a whole lot more came out.

Whether you're recovering from a shart escape, trying to contain a disaster in progress, or just fighting residual funk, this section is about keeping your car from reminding you of your defeat.

There are some basics that you should always have in your car, not only for sharting emergencies, but for emergencies in general. While you don't need to demonstrate the level of paranoia that leads to MRE rations hogging trunk space, there are some helpful things to have on hand.

WIPES

Baby wipes or body wipes are just a good thing to have on hand. Sometimes you might need a quick refresh. If you do have a situation in your pants, they make excellent cleanup tools. Look for brands that are gentle, with helpful ingredients like aloe vera, chamomile, or vitamin E, because they are better for your skin.

TISSUES

From runny stools to runny noses, tissues are always a vital tool. Don't scrimp and buy the cheap ones. If there is anywhere to splurge, it is on high-quality tissue. A tissue with lotion is a good option if you have to wipe sensitive areas often.

HAND SANITIZER

There is no telling what dirty germs you might come in contact with throughout your day, so make sure to have a quality hand sanitizer on hand at all times. Make sure that you get sanitizer that has at least a sixty percent alcohol content. Avoid alcohol free or scented ones that won't do their job.

DISPOSABLE GLOVES

Not only are gloves a good solution in shart situations, but they are also good for other things. Maybe keep them tucked away because the last thing you want your friends to start assuming is that you are frequently in need of a way to hide your fingerprints. Disposable gloves on hand lead to thoughts of moonlighting grave diggers or serial killers.

ESSENTIAL OILS FOR EMERGENCIES

Along with your other supplies, essential oils can be good to keep in the glove box. There are several smells that will help cover and dispel your odorous mistakes. Even if your bottom half has betrayed you, your upper half deserves aromatherapy.

PEPPERMINT OIL

The sharp, fresh smell is great for masking other smells that have more toxic emissions than fresh air. Peppermint oil can also provide relief from nausea if the aroma and stress of the situation are really getting to you.

LAVENDER OIL

Not only can it calm you down in emergency situations, but it also does a great job at masking the cloying poop smell.

TEA TREE OIL

When you are just tired of smelling altogether, tea tree oil can go a long way to overwhelming your olfactory system and forcing it into submission. It can freshen fabrics, like car upholstery, on the microbial level.

LEMON OIL

Try to bring a little optimism into play with lemon oil. It can remind you of clean bathrooms—something you should have found earlier. It is a wonderful, bright, cheerful smell that will help make you feel clean again.

WHAT IS THE BEST OPTION QUIZ

Take a look at these scenarios to see if you are prepared for a worst-case smell scenario.

SCENARIO ONE:

You're in the carpool lane with co-workers when what was supposed to be a quiet relief comes out with more than expected. The windows are rolled up, and the smell is moving fast. You have ten seconds. Quick, what do you do?

A. Crack a window and blame it on the exhaust pipe.

B. Dive for your emergency peppermint oil and rub it under your nose while ignoring everyone else's shock.

C. Spray glittery body mist everywhere and pray for forgiveness as you blind the driver.

D. Yell, "SKUNK!" and hope everyone buys it.

SCENARIO TWO:

You are at a work meeting with several of the most important people in the company. A future promotion is on the line between you and your work rival. Suddenly, your stomach rumbles and hot lava squirts out your butt. The smell is horrific. What should you do?

A. Stand up slowly, grab your bag with wipes and body spray, and make a discreet exit.

B. Stay seated and try to fan the air with your notepad, while looking innocent.

C. Loudly accuse the intern of "eating too many eggs again."

D. Throw your coffee on the floor and shout, "I spilled! I have to leave!"

SCENARIO THREE:

After a good workout, you are wearing light colored leggings. You thought it was just a little gas working its way out after those burpees. It isn't. It is much more. What now?

A. Use your long cardigan or jacket to cover the back, tie it tight, and head to the restroom with dignity.

B. Rub a dryer sheet on your backside and hope for an instant miracle. That's what they are supposed to do, right?

C. Duck into a store, buy glitter spray, and try to "bedazzle the disaster."

D. Lie on your stomach and crawl to the exit, avoid eye contact, and say nothing. Everyone will forget you were there.

SCENARIO FOUR:

While leaving a building, you decide to take the elevator because you've already gotten enough steps in for the day. Suddenly, you realize you've let loose a stench that is offensive to every nose, and people are looking around. What's your best next step?

A. Casually open your purse, pull out a tissue with lemon oil, and discreetly dab your collar, maybe waft it around a little bit.

B. Begin looking around frantically and ask if anyone else "smells that ghost."

C. Fake a sneeze so you can aggressively spritz air freshener into the air like a shaman and ignore the puzzled looks.

D. Cry. Just cry. Loudly and wetly. Own nothing. You don't know these people.

SCENARIO FIVE

You are on a first date, and while trying to get comfortable in the tiny bistro seat, you suddenly realize there is a squishiness that shouldn't be there. What's your only hope?

A. Excuse yourself calmly and take your bag with the emergency kit inside to the restroom. Hopefully, you'll be able to stop the disaster before it hits the outer layers, so you don't have to explain color-changing pants.

B. Pull out vodka spray and mist yourself while saying, "I'm not like other people you've dated."

C. End the date early with a dramatic, "I just remembered I left my oven on." Block their number and never mention the date to anyone.

D. Pull out your dry shampoo, shake it into your lap, and declare you're "fighting thigh humidity."

SCENARIO SIX

You're in the middle of a wedding ceremony—front row, right behind Grandma—when your stomach betrays you with a surprise eruption. The vows pause, heads turn, and the bride looks directly at you. What's your move?

A. Whisper "Excuse me," and quietly exit the pew, get cleaned up, and stay in the reception area until people start exiting. Just join the flow.

B. Drop your program on the floor, dive under the pew, and stay there until the reception.

C. Clutch your stomach, mutter "The spirit is moving," and let the preacher redirect attention back to holy matters.

D. Fan the air with the hymnal like you're worshipping extra hard to make the air flow, disperse the smell, and spread the blame.

If you find yourself never knowing what the best answer is, go back and reread the chapters so far. And know that at no point is glitter spray the answer. In fact, if you reach for glitter spray to solve any problems, know that you are a hazard.

If you answered all A's, then you are on track to maintain your dignity and reputation no matter the situation. Congratulations, you have taken the advice you've received so far and made it work for you.

If you got some right and some wrong, no worries—there is hope for you yet. Maybe as you continue to learn more, you'll start to have a better understanding of this perfectly human and perfectly horrible condition. Being prepared is not just about making sure you know what to do next. It is also about being confident.

[5]
CONFIDENCE REBUILDING
& MENTAL RECOVERY

Once your day has turned sh*tty, there is nothing to do but pull up your squishy pants and carry on. Knowing how to rebuild your confidence, laugh through the worst of it, and recover after the situation is just as important as knowing what to do when it happens.

Yes, This Happened. No, You're Not Alone

The stigma that surrounds farting, pooping, and the dreaded shart? One hundred percent man-made. Humans decided somewhere along the way that a butt misfire meant moral failure. It's just humans who have taken this perfectly natural body function and turned it into a social taboo. The rest of the natural world is out there treating poop like it's no big deal. Some creatures proudly wear it, sniff it, or raise families in it. They embrace it, just like you are going to have to.

Elephants are majestic creatures that are iconic for being smart, wise, and having long memories. Elephants are considered one of the most intelligent animals on the planet because of their complex brains. Videos of them using tools to problem-solve and show empathy to their fellow animals are popular.

What you might not have realized is that they are very pro-poo. Baby elephants, those cute, clumsy babies, eat adult poop. It's because they need the gut microbes that are in the adult's stomach. Without those microbes, the elephants wouldn't be able to digest their vegetable diet. The babies are born without those important microbes and can't get them from milk, so their only source is adult elephant poop.

Man's and woman's best friends are known for their companionship and the wonderful joy they bring to life. These furry family members can't be replaced, and know only how to love, but despite their amazing attributes, we don't like to talk about their love of something else.

52

Dogs sniff poop to learn about other dogs and leave it as a calling card. Their poop can tell about age, gender, health, and sometimes even the territory. If smelling it isn't enough, they like to plop down and roll around in the poop. Really gets the smells out there. And probably an owner's favorite doggie habit is coprophagia, also known as eating poop. Dog poop, cat poop, mystery poop, around twenty-five percent of dogs have done it. More probably would if we stopped yelling at them.

To really understand how helpful poop can be, let's take a look at bunnies. The soft, fluffy spokesperson animal for Easter is hiding a shameful secret. Beyond those adorable, silky ears, cute, cotton tail, and precious, tiny paws is a side of bunnies that no one wants to talk about. And the Easter Bunny wants to be kept on the down-low.

Rabbits produce nutrient-rich feces called cecotropes, which they ingest directly from their butt. These soft, nutrient-rich droppings, produced through fermentation in the cecum, are re-ingested to get additional vitamins and proteins that weren't absorbed during the first pass through. This process is crucial for rabbits to thrive on their high-fiber diet.

These are just some of the animals that have embraced their feces for the gift it is. So, if you've had an unfortunate accident, just think like an elephant and keep going. Be like a bird—they poop and keep flying.

LAUGHTER IS
THE BEST MEDICINE:

The shame that sharting carries comes from the silence that we have allowed to grow around these so-called accidents. Sometimes the trick is to know how to own your shame and turn it into a makeshift comedy routine.

TRY OUT SOME OF THESE ONE-LINERS:

- You know what that fart and your last relationship had in common? We had to force them, and they were both full of crap.
- They say don't trust a fart after forty. Well, it turns out you shouldn't trust one after tacos, either.
- That was a tactical error. And now it's a logistical nightmare. Excuse me.
- That fart was like our Monday meetings—completely unnecessary and made everyone uncomfortable
- Like my diet, it started with good intentions and ended in disaster.
- That was my digestive system rage-quitting in real time.
- Excuse me, that shart was like a bad plot twist—nobody saw it coming, and now we all regret it.
- Sorry, that was my a** hitting "reply all" when it should've been a private message.

It takes a certain amount of flair to make a joke out of sharting, and maybe you can get away with just making a joke about farts. No need to claim the shart if you can get away with a slightly less embarrassing fart.

No matter what humor you decide to use, be humble and prepared to leave the area quickly.

SHARING THE STORY
(BUT ONLY IF YOU OWN IT)

Sometimes the best way to take some sting out of an embarrassing situation is to be able to share and laugh about it. If you can tell the story and have other people commiserate with you, it goes a long way to making the situation less . . . volatile.

Before sharing your story, make sure you are ready. If, when you try to think about the incident, you are having a sweaty, heart-pounding flashback, it is still too early to be making jokes about it. When you reach the point that you are genuinely ready to laugh about it, then you'll know you are ready to share.

Make sure you share the story in the appropriate setting. Places you shouldn't talk about sharting, or really any embarrassing or poop stories, would include places like:

> **Job interviews.** That isn't your best "I overcame a challenge" story. I promise.

> **First dates.** While accidents and embarrassing stories are part of a true relationship, they might not need to be the foundation you try to start one on.

> **Wedding toast.** Don't ruin someone's magical day with a story of your least magical day.

> **Family meals.** Not everyone has a stomach strong enough to handle a shart story while trying to enjoy their turkey.

> **In court.** While putting your hand on a bible and swearing to tell the truth can be scary, they don't need that much truth.

Having the right setting is essential to retelling your story. A more intimate friend's night in or chill time would be the place to bust out your soul-crushing truth.

Know your audience and don't overshare to the point people are leaving, trying to avoid hearing the gory details. Also, don't tell other people's stories. Don't talk about someone else's mishap, and don't talk about anyone that might have been accidentally included in yours. Making fun of yourself to move on is fine. Making fun of others is not.

HOW TO RE-ENTER SOCIETY AFTER A PUBLIC MISHAP

If you have to return to the scene of the crime, give yourself at least twenty-four hours. The twenty-four hours will give you time to recollect yourself, your dignity, and for everyone else to recover.

The best method that you and hopefully everyone else can employ is the "Act Like Nothing Happened" (ALNH) method. The ALNH method has saved many people from embarrassing situations that they didn't know how to handle.

You have to be able to come into the room with your head held high, the same as any other day. If anyone tries to bring up the horrifying subject, just calmly tell them, "It was unfortunate, but I've chosen not to discuss it." This lets everyone know that you have opted for the ALNH method, and as part of polite society, they should as well.

While this won't stop people from gossiping and giggling behind closed doors or in the other room, it does prevent you from having to relive the embarrassment and shame.

If someone does choose to ignore polite procedures and continues to bring it up, ask them bluntly if there is a reason they are so interested in your pants' situation. Have they recently experienced a similar situation?

The threat of sharing in the shame will encourage people to move along. And chances are, they probably did have a similar situation at some point in their life.

It might be a good idea to let the pants in question go to the dumpster. No need to wear something that will remind everyone of the redecorating you did. Instead of seeing an awesome pair of pants, they'll just be reminded of the gooey mess you had to handle.

SURVIVING GROUP TEXTS & SOCIAL MEDIA

If you are part of an active online or chat group that you know will never stay quiet on the subject, don't be scared to be the first to bring it up. Make the narrative what you want it to be. If you treat it like a joke, then when the story gets to be too much, it is okay to walk away from your haters. Mute their chat or delete their comments. You don't have to give online bullies a front row seat and let them run the show.

No one has to be part of your social media life or have access to your text messages. Block people. If someone has nothing but negativity to bring into your life, you don't need them. Surround yourself with people who make you feel good about yourself, in real life and digitally.

Ask a trusted friend or family member to jump on social media and come to your defense. When your bullies realize that not everyone thinks it is funny to pick on someone for digestive failure, they might move along. Even if they don't, having positive comments will encourage other people to be understanding and uplifting.

If discouraging anyone from digitally bullying you doesn't work, understand that silence is golden. Focus on your real life and stay away from social media and your phone for a while. The chances are you spend too much time on them, anyway.

Any bullies will move along faster when you don't interact with them. It's only fun to be a bully when you are getting a reaction, so don't provide one. Always remember, your a** might have failed you, but at least you aren't one. Leave the people who are alone.

BUILDING THE MENTAL FORTITUDE OF A TRUE SURVIVOR

Once you've had a life-altering, embarrassing situation, it can tear away at your confidence. Having the mental fortitude to overcome this newest challenge will help you be a better person.

Before or after your sharting experience, you should embrace daily affirmations.

- "I am more than my mistakes."
- "My worth isn't defined by other people's opinions."
- "Today I'll get a little bit stronger and grow my confidence."
- "I will remember progress over perfection."
- "My greatest strength is _____."
- "I am in control of my reactions, if not my circumstances."

Those are all great ways to start your day, repeating them to yourself over and over until you truly believe them. You can also add to them to help you work toward your goals.

After sharting, your daily affirmations might need to sound different for a while, or at least until you manage to overcome the horror and rebuild your confidence.

- "I survived. Not my pants, but I did survive."
- "One accident does not define my life."
- "Everyone has a story, and it is okay that mine has poop in it."
- "I am not the first, and I will not be the last."
- "My confidence can be stain-resistant."
- "Every day I can wake up poop free is a good day."

Whatever you need to tell yourself to make it better. Make this new power statement the first thing you say in the morning, and the last thing you say at night. It will eventually become true.

You have to keep everything in perspective. Somewhere in the world right now, someone is sharting themselves. At least you aren't doing it again. Say a quick prayer for the person living your nightmare in real time and move on with your life.

If you find that you are easily embarrassed, you might want to desensitize yourself. Try completing micro-dares throughout your day. Little actions that will embarrass you just a bit. Like wearing mismatched socks, making random dad jokes to strangers, singing a song in an elevator, or asking random people questions about themselves.

Getting used to being slightly off beat will help you avoid getting as upset about large, embarrassing situations, and eventually the misadventure in your pants will seem like nothing.

CONFIDENCE HACKS FOR YOUR NEXT PUBLIC APPEARANCE

After your shartpocalypse, it can be difficult to make that next public appearance. All kinds of fears are running through your head: Will it happen again? Will someone who knows what happened be there? Or will the closest bathroom be closed?

Take a few simple steps to make it easier. Wear dark pants because even if the unbelievable happens, you'll have some cover and be less exposed. If that doesn't make you feel better, go ahead and whip out your favorite outfit, whether it is a power suit or a sparkly skirt. Wearing something that you love will make you feel better, and maybe your butt will be less likely to mess it up.

Go ahead and look up the bathroom locations. Many venues and places have online maps. If you are concerned, knowing where a quick escape is will save you anxiety. Save the map on your phone or print it out to tuck away in your bag. Plus, your friends will be really impressed when, as they wander aimlessly, you whip out a map and lead the group.

When you arrive somewhere new, go ahead and start the conversations. No need to dwell on your fears, and being a leader builds confidence. Confidence will drown out your fears, and that voice in your head imagining the worst-case scenario. If you aren't in a position to start conversations, try the two-second rule. Make eye contact with people and smile for two seconds.

Choose a fragrance that you love. If you don't smell like poop, you'll be less likely to think about it. Better to leave a lingering scent of citrus or jasmine behind you when you walk away than a lingering odor of rotting sewage. Knowing you are leaving a good scent behind will give you the confidence to move on with poise.

TURNING TRAGEDY INTO TRIUMPH

If no matter what you do, the terrible tragedy just won't go away, and it is what you'll be forever remembered for, go ahead and embrace it. There are worse things to be remembered for than having a loose bowel.

Name the event. Commemorate the episode. Go big or go home. Make the retelling of your story sound like the first part of an epic saga. Names like The Great Taco Tragedy, The Walmart Washout, The Mudslide of Midtown, or whatever great name works for you.

Take the next step if you want and give yourself an epic name too. Nobody is going to forget The Lord of the Rumbles, The Sultan of Splatter, Empress of Eruptions, or whatever name you feel captures you.

If you have truly managed to come up with an epic name for the incident or title for yourself, go ahead and have T-shirts made. Cool graphics and sayings like "Survivor of the Great Taco Tragedy" will go a long way to making you a legend that everyone will talk about at the next grill out.

Handled right, it also takes care of the next Christmas gifts for friends and family. T-shirts that say "I know The Lord of the Rumbles" or "I witnessed The Walmart Washout" can be proudly worn by your friends and family who want to be part of the legend.

CHOOSING AN EPIC NAME: LEGENDS DESERVE TITLES

STEP ONE: PICK YOUR POWER WORD

These are your "epic" openers:

- Lord/Lady
- Sultan/Queen
- Captain/Commander
- Empress/Emperor
- Duke/Duchess
- Master/Mistress
- Guardian/Warden

Your Power Word:

STEP TWO: PICK YOUR CATASTROPHE

- Rumbles
- Splatter
- Storms
- Eruptions
- Thunderpants
- Backdraft
- The Brownout
- Quake
- Boom

Your Catastrophe:

STEP THREE: ADD YOUR TWIST

Give your name extra punch with something that makes it uniquely you:

- A location (of the Gas Station Restroom, of Aisle 5).
- A date or event (of New Year's Eve, of The County Fair).
- A descriptive flair (the Unstoppable, the Slightly Unhinged, the Unflushed).
- A mysterious title (the Unknown, the Whispered One).
- A personal inside joke (of Aunt Linda's House, of The Road Trip).

Your Twist:

STEP FOUR: COMBINE & CLAIM IT

Mix your chosen words into your Official Epic Name:

- Lord of the Rumbles
- Empress of Eruptions
- Captain Backdraft of Midtown
- Duchess Thunderpants the Fearless

Write it here, big and bold:

STEP FIVE: BONUS POINTS

Say it out loud in your most dramatic movie-trailer voice to everyone you see.

Tell a friend. Explain that this is how you should be referred to now, and see if they salute you, bow, or laugh.

Optional merch: put it on a mug, T-shirt, or phone case. It is not official until it is in print.

[6]
PREVENTION & GUT PREPAREDNESS PLANNING

Taking care of your gut and gut health is a vital tool in your anti-shart kit. A gut that is running well is less likely to have accidents. When you take care of your gut health, your gut will take care of you.

HYDRATION & FIBER: YOUR GUT'S SECRET WEAPONS

Your gut health can affect every part of your life. It affects your digestion, nutrient absorption, immunity, and will even affect your mental health.

Without a healthy gut, your body isn't able to correctly absorb the nutrients you are eating. Not having the proper nutrients can lead to a compromised immune system. Without a strong immune system, you'll wind up catching every germ, virus, or plague that dances by.

Beyond keeping you healthy, the gut microbiome affects your mood, emotions, and even your cognitive functions. Some studies have gone so far as to link bad gut health with anxiety, depression, and even autism. While science continues to evolve with more studies, your gut microbiome appears to be gaining importance, not losing it. As you age, maintaining good gut health can help prevent and reduce diseases, such as autoimmune disorders, heart disease, and certain types of cancer.

One of the easiest things to do when you are looking to improve your gut health is to increase your fiber intake. Fiber passes through your digestive system and can help remove toxins as it travels.

Fiber also adds to your stool, keeping everything moving like it is supposed to. Avoiding constipation can help prevent unexpected blowouts. Being regular is an integral part of avoiding sharts.

Another benefit of fiber is its ability to act as a prebiotic, helping the beneficial gut microbes thrive. While helping the good bacteria thrive, fiber can also keep your body from absorbing some cholesterol in other foods. Keeping your cholesterol absorption down can help with heart health and blood pressure.

If you have a history of diabetes, fiber will help improve your blood sugar level and slow the absorption of unhealthy sugars. Higher-fiber diets have also been linked to a healthy weight. Increasing your fiber intake has a range of benefits, the least of which is preventing sharts.

Water is also crucial because it acts as a lubricant and helps break down food. When in your body, it can help dissolve minerals and nutrients from your food so that your body will absorb them. If you don't like water and find yourself having a hard time drinking it, just remember that your future pants will thank you!

By simply making sure to eat at least twenty-five grams of fiber a day as a woman, and thirty-five grams a day as a man, you can make huge improvements in your health. Especially when combined with twelve cups of water a day for women, and sixteen cups a day for men.

KNOW YOUR TRIGGERS

Food tracking is an excellent tool if you are unsure about food sensitivity or why your stomach might occasionally act up. Not only does food tracking help pinpoint problem foods, but it can also increase your awareness of what you are consuming, which is beneficial for your overall health.

Start keeping a food journal. It doesn't have to be a special one; simply record all the food you eat throughout the day, as well as any liquids you consume. At the end of each day, tally up your total fiber and water to make sure you are staying on track. Record how you have felt throughout the day, any bowel movements, and your gas level. Consider this new journal your *Book of Intestinal Prophecy*.

After spending several weeks tracking, you can start to see patterns about which foods make you feel bad, upset your stomach, or cause gassiness. Once you identify the problem foods, it is easier to avoid them, unless you are at home with some time to kill.

Dairy can cause an upset stomach to anyone who is lactose intolerant. Different people have different tolerance levels, and you might find that having a coffee with cream can leave you in trouble, or you might be able to eat a pound of cheese before your stomach starts rebelling.

While many people love spicy food, it may actually be contributing to your gastrointestinal distress. Spicy food contains capsaicin, which has been shown to trigger pain receptors in your digestive tract. Every person has different tolerance levels to capsaicin. You might find you have a stomach of steel or need to steer clear of all spice when in public.

Greasy foods are harder to digest than other foods. The fat, which is the grease, is a slowly digested macronutrient, forcing your digestive system to work harder. The slow digestion prevents food from leaving your body at a rapid pace, and excessive greasy food leaves your digestive system unable to keep up. Undigested fat acts as a laxative, causing diarrhea.

You might consider it a morning necessity, but coffee could also be adding to your tummy trouble. Coffee has a stimulating effect. The caffeine stimulates the central nervous system and triggers the stomach to produce more hydrochloric acid. The acid irritates the stomach lining and can cause loose stools to escape unexpectedly.

Pay attention so you can learn what works for you, and what could lead to a socially destructive faux pas.

CHOOSING SAFE FOODS BEFORE DATES & PUBLIC EVENTS

If you are planning to attend an important event, a big outing, or a large gathering, the last thing you need is a shart destroying your plans. There are some foods that you can eat that might prevent your worst nightmare from becoming the most memorable event.

Try switching to gentle on the gut foods and save yourself the embarrassment. No matter how much you love hot wings, they might not love you. Skip your favorite meal before a big date because you want to have love in the air, not mystery fumes.

There is no faster way to destroy romance than to rush to the bathroom mid-sentence. You are looking for butterflies in your stomach, not your last meal trying to forcibly exit. Try eating foods from the low FODMAP diet.

Low FODMAP is a temporary diet that can help you manage gut issues. FODMAP is fermentable, oligosaccharides (fructans and galactans), disaccharides (lactose), monosaccharides (fructose), and polyols (sugar alcohols). The goal of the low FODMAP is to avoid all those potentially gut-upsetting foods.

Some proteins that are well-cooked and low-fat can be good to enjoy with your plain grains and starches. Some skinless chicken breast or ground turkey can be tasty without leaving you concerned. White fish, eggs, and tofu are all good choices too. If you find that your food is tasteless, try marinating it in lemon juice and olive oil.

Some vegetables are safe to eat, like zucchini, green beans, bok choy, carrots, cucumbers, potatoes, tomatoes, and lettuce. Enjoy the veggies in salads, soups, stir-fries, roasted, or even raw in wraps and sandwiches. Vegetables pack a punch when it comes to flavor and nutrients.

There are some fruits you can enjoy as well, like cantaloupe, grapes, pineapple, blueberries, strawberries, oranges, kiwi, and bananas. For any food, no matter how low FODMAP, you need to make sure you are only eating a serving because overeating will lead to the same problems you are trying to avoid.

Other foods you can enjoy include hard cheese, almond milk, oats, sourdough bread, wheat-free breads, and rice cakes.

Not all foods are the same, so avoid garlic, onions, cabbage, watermelon, apples, breaded foods, almonds, pizza, and anything that has lactose if you are following the low FODMAP diet.

BATHROOM SCHEDULES

A bathroom schedule is a preplanned outline for when to use the toilet for both number one and two. You were probably on a bathroom schedule when you were a child learning to use the toilet.

If you want to start a bathroom schedule, just map out when you are most likely to have to use the restroom, like after waking up, after meals, before activities, and at regular intervals.

The hope is that if you are on a bathroom schedule, you won't have unexpected surprises trickling or exploding into your undies.

Pros of a bathroom schedule include a reassuring level of predictability. You won't find yourself in dire need of a commode, with none in sight. This predictability can reduce your anxiety about bathroom-related issues. It might not reduce the anxiety in your relationship, but you'll have fewer toilet worries.

Making sure that you are consistently emptying your bowels can lead to better gut health and make for smoother days. If you have ever had explosive diarrhea in a public bathroom while the person in the next stall coughs awkwardly, you'll know it can ruin your day.

While a bathroom schedule seems like the best thing ever, there are some cons to the habit. It is not always practical, especially if you work, travel, or just live life. There might not always be a bathroom break at the exact same time every day.

You also might find that some trips are a waste of time because you don't have to go. If you have a full schedule, every wasted minute might put you farther behind. It might also be awkward to have to interrupt a conversation when an alarm goes off, saying, *Excuse me, the lavatory awaits.*

On the other hand, you might have to limit your food or water intake; otherwise, you'll never make it to the next scheduled bathroom break.

Look at your lifestyle and decide if a bathroom schedule would help or hinder you in your attempt to keep your gut happy and your sharts to a minimum.

PREEMPTIVE BATHROOM VISITS

Schedule or no schedule, preemptively visiting the bathroom can be a game-changer. If you are getting ready to embark on a long road trip, a probably tedious meeting, an exciting once-in-a-lifetime concert, or a bumpy flight, take the time to go to the bathroom before you get started.

Visit the restroom, have a seat, and wait a bit. You might be surprised at what comes out. Our body is trained to go to the bathroom when we sit on the toilet. You can trigger a lot of bowel movements by tricking your brain into thinking it needs to go now.

If it is an extremely high-risk event coming up, go ahead and chill on the throne twice. Maybe you do something twice, or maybe not. Just give yourself peace of mind knowing you did everything you could. It is better to waste those few minutes beforehand than have to give up an hour later getting cleaned up. An ounce of prevention is worth a pound of laundry detergent.

SAFE ZONES: BATHROOMS YOU SHOULD KNOW IN EVERY BUILDING

There are public bathrooms everywhere, but we all know some are better than others. You might not be at the point of keeping notebooks of bathrooms with your own personalized rating system, but it never hurts to know which bathrooms are best, and which ones to avoid — avoid — avoid.

Anytime you can find a *single-occupancy bathroom,* it is the best choice. There is nothing finer than privacy on a loo outside of your house. The door will lock, they are often cleaner, there's plenty of room for any bags, and they're great for a loud relief. They might be difficult to find, and can have a line, so they won't always be an option, but keep an eye out in case you get lucky.

A good low-traffic bathroom is the *employee bathroom.* You'll have to find someone who works at the establishment and ask for permission, but if you can manage to get it, employee-only bathrooms are the way to go. The employee bathrooms see less traffic and tend to be better cleaned. If you are told no, accept it with grace and move on, but it never hurts to ask. If you are an employee, just assume you can use it, and if you are told you can't find another job.

Hotel bathrooms are an often-overlooked option. If you are out and about looking for a bathroom, check out the hotels in the area. Most hotels have bathrooms in the lobby, and they are always well-maintained, clean, and well-stocked. Unless it is peak check-in time, there is low foot traffic in a hotel lobby. Avoid times like three to four o'clock, when the majority of the guests are checking in.

It's important to be considerate when looking for a bathroom — especially when visiting a new location, regardless of the type of business.

Depending on where you are, *office building bathrooms* can be hit or miss. Nicer offices and businesses will have better facilities, but you have to go hunt for the bathrooms that are hidden. Don't trust the bathroom off the main strip because it will be well-used and public.

If you have the time, take a look around and explore your bathroom options, rather than settling for the first toilet you come across.

PRE-FART WARM-UPS: TEST RELEASES

A test release is an important safety check. These trial toots can save your pants and your dignity. While not foolproof, they can help you gauge just how much distress your intestines are in.

The first step is to do a pressure reading. Once you have done a quick recon of the area and find yourself safely spaced away from everyone else, check the pressure level. If you feel an insane amount of buildup, then abort. Nothing good will come from letting that pressure be released in a public place.

If you feel like the pressure isn't too much, then try out a small "toot trial." Once again, stop and survey the area because you don't want to have any witnesses, no matter how it goes. If your stomach has a lot of gurgling going on, you need to abort and head to the bathroom.

Attempt a slow leak to release pressure. Think of a balloon that is slowly releasing air. If you are having trouble releasing the air, try tilting to one side and maybe reaching back and pulling a cheek to the side. This will give the air a free escape and hopefully reduce sound.

If you aren't where you can find a quiet, isolated place, try using a micro-fart in motion technique. Release small toots as you walk and move away from the area. Leave the people there blaming each other for any smells that are escaping.

Being aware of your surroundings is very important if you are attempting to release a quick test to determine where people are around you and be prepared if you leave an odor behind. Don't use an elevator as your testing ground. Yes, even if you are alone. No, you will not be able to explain the smell when you exit the elevator.

HOW TO TRUST (OR NOT TRUST) A SILENT FART

While there is no way to guarantee a silent fart, using your test releases will go a long way toward telling you what you're dealing with. If the pre-test run doesn't go well, there is a very high chance that your full release will not go well. Best to head to the bathroom.

One way to hedge your bets is to take some basic precautions in case the silent fart is not so silent. Look at your environment. If you are standing on the carpet—excellent. Carpet is a natural sound absorber, which means that when the loud air rushes from your bum, the sound will be stopped by the carpet, instead of being sent on.

Carpet absorbs sound waves so that they don't bounce off because it is soft and porous. Fiber traps and dissipates sound energy. Hardwood or tile floors are not good release grounds. If you are standing on a hard surface, go find somewhere else to release your gas back into the wild.

Hardwoods, tile, and any other solid hard surface won't absorb the sound wave but instead will bounce them off and send them on. Think about standing in a cave and yelling; how the sound would travel as it echoes. Now think about standing in a hallway and having your supposedly silent fart echoing down so that everyone else in the hallway can hear it too. Nightmares have been crafted from less.

For all that is holy, don't try to slip a fart out while sitting on a metal chair. It is likely to vibrate, alerting everyone near, and echo to alert everyone afar.

If you are around people, remember that sound can be your friend. Loud places like concerts or the stock exchange floor are a wonderful place to let loose some of that buildup. You might not be able to stop the smell, but no one will hear a thing. If you are sitting in church, there isn't enough prayer to stop the congregation from hearing you let one rip during the scripture reading.

Using a fart warm-up and situational awareness, you can be pretty confident in your silent fart (even if it turns out not to be). However, there are some situations where you simply need to excuse yourself or hold it. If you are on a plane, in a classroom, leading a meeting, or anywhere else, you can't make an escape if things go horribly wrong. So, think long and hard.

[7]
ADVANCED SURVIVAL STRATEGIES

Sometimes the basics just don't cover it, and you need to have some advanced strategies in place. There is no shame in being prepared, but there is plenty of shame in getting called out for sharting in a room full of people.

TACTICAL EXITS: LEAVING A ROOM WITHOUT AROUSING SUSPICION

When the time comes, you will need to quickly escape a room before anyone notices that you've had an "uh-oh," there are some ways to make the escape, I mean exit, happen smoothly.

Keep your shoes tied. If you have laces and try to exit gracefully, nothing ruins it faster than face-planting in your hurry. When you hit the ground, more than likely, the floodgates are going to open up. You'll be left face down with a disgraced butt in the air.

Don't forget, when you are at work, supplies are often left unstocked. No one wants to make the extra trip to restock the staples, tape, and pens. Be the office hero and use it as a way to leave the room quickly. Just announce, "Excuse me while I go get us some more copy paper."

When all else fails, use man's fear of illness to escape the room. Start coughing uncontrollably and wave your hand around. This will cause people to back up and understand you are going to do... something. The hand won't be clear, but that is okay. It will get you out of the room.

If you find that you don't care to come up with cliché excuses and want to be above all mundane concerns, there is a great way to do that. Simply lift one eyebrow and smirk. Shake your head slightly and leave the room without a word. People will assume that you have much more important matters to attend to, and hopefully, never realize it is the turd in your pants.

Most people have an undying love for animals, so use it to your advantage by looking at your phone and then announcing, "Oh no, my sweet (insert pet name) has gotten into (something dangerous around your house). I've got to go." If you don't have a pet, no worries, you now have an imaginary one that can be used for many excuses in years to come.

Having no pets and not having an interest in keeping up with an imaginary one doesn't mean that you can't use the animal excuse to your advantage. Let people know that you are running to recycle or to volunteer at a shelter. No one will question a thing.

THE "BLAME THE BABY" MANEUVER

If you are fortunate enough to have access to a real baby, then you are in excuse heaven. No one doubts the stink bomb those little booties can deliver. You won't have to take responsibility for your fart, sharts, or any other bodily function until they are old enough to defend themselves.

You let out a silent but deadly one that comes with all the extra toppings? No problem. Loudly announce to the surrounding area, "Oh no, diaper emergency!"

No need to explain that you might be the one who needs a diaper, not the baby.

Really, you don't even have to use words. You can just vaguely wave some wipes around while smiling apologetically, and no one even doubts what happened.

If anyone looks at you sideways, just politely tell them it is teething gas. Nobody should think twice about a medical excuse. After all, that noxious smell wafting from the two of you has to have a medical reason to be that toxic.

What if you don't have a bouncing bundle of joy with you to blame the incident on? Or what if there is no bouncing bundle of joy at all? You can still use the baby diversion method effectively.

When a smell starts emanating from your vicinity, look in your bag and loudly exclaim, "How did that dirty diaper get in here? Darn kids." Every parent in the area will nod knowingly, and the non-parents will be too grossed out to ask any questions.

For extra protection, stick a Baby on Board sticker to your bag. You won't even have to say anything. Many people will look and wince in sympathy before moving on with life.

THE BACKPACK BUFFER: CARRY A BAG FOR STRATEGIC COVERAGE

On days when you aren't sure what to expect and suspect your body might betray you, come prepared. Even if you don't normally carry anything extra, today is not the day to stick to your minimalist ideals.

Backpacks can work as shields in emergencies. If you'll be exposed in a hallway, gathering room, or outside, make sure to have a backpack with you. Once you've sharted yourself, you'll be grateful for that nylon lifesaver. Simply loosen the straps and let it hang down to cover your newly christened derrière.

If backpacks aren't your style, a messenger bag is also a great option. Hanging low enough to rotate and cover your butt, the messenger bag can serve a wide range of uses. It can even double as a seat cover to contain evidence of your shame. A brown, squishy spot where you've been sitting is a dead giveaway.

When carrying a bag, someone might question why you suddenly feel the need to haul luggage around. Let them know you're working to become a more organized individual, prepared for anything the world can throw at you. Pull a planner and a first aid kit out of it to support your story.

While backpacks and messenger bags are both extremely versatile, they aren't the only bag games out there. A laptop case can also work. It is both work-efficient and shame-resistant — sleek enough to carry into a meeting, wide enough to block the view of an unexpected disaster.

For full coverage on a day when you're certain clean pants will be needed, carry two bags. You'll be a full-coverage pro with no worries as you strut away with a laptop case shielding your left cheek and a fully organized messenger bag guarding the right.

WHEN TO FAKE
A PHONE CALL & WALK OUT

There are times it would be rude or inconvenient for you to excuse yourself politely. Those times might call for a sneaky escape that no one can blame you for. Maybe you've sharted or you're about to.

If you find yourself in one of those situations, look no further than your handy, dandy phone to help you extricate yourself. You might not have a lot of time before a massive blowout happens, and a phone is a sure-fire, quick option.

Either you've been out on a date, you know someone who has, or you've seen it on TV, where someone uses the old phone trick to get out. Your phone rings and you answer enthusiastically, "Hey, Mom," then you get serious. "Oh no, how bad is it?" All the while, you are quickly getting your stuff together. And you are talking to John from extended warranty.

You can apply that same technique to escaping to the nearest (or quietest) bathroom. Sometimes you don't even have to answer the phone. Just look down and quickly pick it up before your companions have a chance to see it. "Sorry, I've got a work emergency." Walk out confidently.

Better yet, excuse yourself gravely and walk out nodding and frowning. No one is going to stop you to question what is happening. Unless, of course, you leave an unpaid meal, and then someone is going to question you. Don't dine and dash.

When you are with people that you don't know well, there are even more options to try out. Look down at a "text message" and jump up. "I've got to go; my cat has been run over by a drunk driver." Those people don't know whether you have a cat.

Try setting an alarm. If you find that you are alright with no need for panic, you can just ignore it. But if you find you need a quick escape, jump up and exclaim, "I forgot my medicine." Any person with sense is not going to chase you down to ask about your medical history, and if they do, just tell them it is private. Unless it is a date you are trying to get away from. Then it is your chlamydia medicine.

There are also apps that you can download to call on a schedule. Answer the call like normal, wait a second, and then exclaim, "Freddy swallowed another Lego?" Wave and leave. Nobody has a clue if Freddy is your kid, your roommate, or your dog.

YOU COME BACK
IN DIFFERENT PANTS

After a hazmat event has occurred, you'll find that you need to put on new pants. If you have planned well, you have an identical set in your emergency kit, but very few of us will ever be that prepared when D-day comes.

When you walk back into the room wearing a different pair of pants, some people might have questions. It is a good idea to be prepared to explain whatever pants you wind up wearing, whether they are from your emergency kit, a clothesline you stole them from, or the corner store where you overpaid for them.

SWEATPANTS

It's perfectly reasonable to change into sweatpants. Especially if you are about to eat. You needed the extra room for the meal. Just show off the stretchy waistband, and people will think you are a genius.

YOGA PANTS

Let people know that you are spontaneous. You were thinking about trying out a goat yoga session later on and wanted to go ahead and get your yoga pants stretched out. Nothing worse than goat yoga-ing and realizing your pants weren't ready.

CARGO PANTS

Hey, those pockets are good for a lot of things. You plan to go grocery shopping later and are trying to reduce your plastic bag usage and keep your hands free.

OVERALLS

You planted a garden plot or a container of herbs last week, and now they really speak to you. Show off those handy suspenders. No more belts for you.

LEATHER PANTS

You've got a date later with a motorcyclist and wanted to look the part. No need to give up any skin on the road if the date goes badly. You are smarter than that.

PAJAMA PANTS

Isn't everyone tired of having to dress up for everything? It is time to protest the establishment and demand pajamas on Fridays.

TRACK PANTS

There is supposed to be an ice cream truck in the area, and you are jonesing for some rocky road. Those trucks don't always want to stop, so you are prepared to hunt them down.

HAMMER PANTS

Who doesn't have a little time for "Hammer Time?"

SEQUIN LEGGINGS

The power has been iffy lately, and in case of an outage, you wanted to act as an emergency flare. Plus, who couldn't use more razzle-dazzle in their day?

CAMO PANTS

The apocalypse could happen at any time, and when it does, you have to be ready to go to ground and disappear. If zombies come running down the road, you'll be able to blend in and survive. Everyone better take note and think about their own survival tactic.

KILT

You recently researched your family's ancestry, and now that you know you have a bit of Scottish in you, it is time to embrace your heritage. Plus, it is nice and airy.

FISHING WADERS

You can't trust the weather channel, and your big toe has been throbbing—could mean rain. Better safe than sorry when the streets start flooding.

EXCUSES THAT ACTUALLY WORK (AND WHICH TO AVOID)

There are many excuses that can be used, and some that are just outlandish. Knowing some good excuses is always a good idea. Having some ready to fire out of the cannon at a moment's notice, or a tummy's rumble, is a lifesaver.

Use the tried-and-true work excuse. Most people know bosses are demanding and ungrateful, so it won't be shocking to explain that you are needed in the office or have a last-minute deadline you completely forgot about. Add a little aggravation and resignation to the mix, and you'll be gold.

Many people suffer from a wide range of medical problems, so it isn't surprising when someone has to leave unexpectedly because of one. Avoid saying, "Sorry, I have to leave because molten lava just shot out my a**," and try instead, "Sorry, I just got the worst migraine. I'll have to reschedule."

You can always go with a softer version of the truth. Let your companion know that the shrimp you had for lunch might be fighting back, so you want to head home. Don't tell them the shrimp is MMA fighting its way out of your exit hatch. Just a gentle nod to the problem and off you go.

On the way to an engagement, you can stall for time if you are in cleanup mode. The tried and true, "I've got a flat," will do the job, with no embellishment needed. Everyone has a flat tire at some point if they drive and understand the knuckle-busting job that is now required. Or how long it takes for a tow truck to come handle it for you.

Knowing what bad excuses sound like is also important. The last thing you want to do is fire off what you think is a genius cover and realize later you sounded like a moron.

Don't use off-the-wall excuses like, "I need to go feed my sourdough starter." That is not an emergency. That is a poorly thought-out attempt at escape, and you aren't fooling anyone.

"I've been kidnapped." That is not a reason for being late; that is a reason for being in the news headlines. And if you don't show up on the five o'clock news, people are going to realize you were a big, fat liar. As a rule of thumb, avoid excuses that get news coverage.

"The aliens are watching me." The goal is to get out of public humiliation, not wind up in a padded room. If your excuse sounds worse than, "I sharted my pants," just go with the truth. It is easier to accept a stomach mishap than aliens are among us.

Know your audience, because the person you are trying to avoid will help you decide which excuses are perfect and which should be left in the twilight zone.

DEPLOYING A FRIEND AS A DISTRACTION OR COVER

Go out with a true, blue friend; the kind you tell everything to. You're never really alone. Having a best friend with you can make getting out of a compromising situation even easier. Two is better than one when it comes to the art of distraction. They'll be your ultimate partner in crime.

A best friend knows your signals, your panicked face, and exactly when to swoop in with a well-timed "emergency text." They're the kind of person who doesn't just cover for you. They sell the cover story like an Oscar nominee. With a wingman like that, you're not just escaping embarrassment, you're pulling off a heist-level getaway.

Abruptly, you realize your pants are full and you are in a ton of crap, literally. Have an emergency code for your best buddy. Let them know that you sure would like to "see a shooting star tonight." And prepare. That's their code word for dumping a drink straight in your lap. It was an accident, so sorry. No worries, you'll just have to go home and change. You can both escape, victorious.

A good friend knows that sometimes they have to take the lesser of embarrassment so that you can avoid a bigger embarrassment. Should you find yourself stuck in the corner trying to hide your embarrassment and shame, a good friend will know it is time to take the plunge. Find something unexpected and loud to trip over. Make the scene as dramatic as possible to give you time to escape.

The kind of friend that you can't replace is the one who knows when DEFCON 5 is needed. There is no escape; you are cornered, smelly, and about to be exposed. Only one option is left. Pull the fire alarm. You both can escape in the crowd and hope you don't run into the fire marshal on the way out.

BUILDING YOUR SECRET CODE SYSTEM

Here are some great ideas for you and your close friends to share. These basic communication skills will help you navigate scary situations, but don't share them with everyone; otherwise, they won't be helpful.

PHYSICAL GESTURES

- Ear Tug → "I need a quick cover story."
- Adjust Glasses → "Get ready to block for me."
- Tap Nose Twice → "Danger level rising—prep an exit plan."
- Drop Napkin/Utensil → "Make a distraction NOW."
- Cross Arms Suddenly → "Deploy the fake emergency text."
- Scratch Head → "Tell everyone I forgot something important."
- Clutch Stomach → "It's happening—clear me a path."
- Point at Watch → "Start the 'urgent appointment' excuse."

- Yawn and Stretch → "Pretend we're leaving together naturally."
- Two Sneezes in a Row → "This is DEFCON 4—prep to evacuate."

VERBAL CODE PHRASES

- "Shooting star" → Ultimate panic signal: spill a drink on me.
- "Time to water the plants" → I need to vanish. Make it believable.
- "Have you seen my keys?" → Start the distraction chatter.
- "I should call my grandma." → Pretend I just got important news.
- "Is it hot in here?" → I need to move toward the exit.
- "Check, please." → We're leaving together, no questions asked.
- "Do you smell popcorn?" → Cover for an odor and get me out.
- "It's taco Tuesday!" → Emergency excuse = food poisoning.
- "Did you see that?" → Look away while I disappear.
- "We should get a picture." → Everyone gathers, I slip out.

OBEJECT-BASED SIGNALS

- Phone on Table Face Down → Text me an excuse immediately.
- Drink Stirring → Start a fake argument to shift focus.
- Napkin on Lap → Napkin on Table → Subtle signal for "Plan B."
- Push Chair Back Suddenly → Create noise/distraction.
- Drop Silverware → Begin chaotic cover.
- Stack Plates Wrong → Time for both of us to "help the waiter."

- Slide Your Backpack Over → Block me as I exit.
- Turn Hat Backward → Initiate full evacuation mode.
- Put on Sunglasses Indoors → Play along with my excuse.
- Flip a Coaster Over → Silent code = rescue mission.

[8]
PUBLIC SHART HORROR STORIES (AND LESSONS LEARNED)

Believe it or not, many people have gone through embarrassing situations and survived to tell the tale. While sharting in public is one of the most embarrassing public shames to survive, it can be done.

Check out the stories that people have lived, survived, and found the courage to share (anonymously, of course).

THE WEDDING TOAST INCIDENT

There is no better event than coming together with college buddies, especially at a wedding. The happiest of occasions, which prove you all made it through college and are building your futures.

Imagine being at a swanky venue, the whole enchilada: white tablecloths, candle lights burning, a champagne fountain flowing, and soft, live music in the background.

I was already nervous because I had been asked to give a toast for the groom. He was one of my oldest friends, and I didn't want to do anything to embarrass him or disappoint him. I desperately wanted the stamp of approval from his new wife and knew that the wedding toast was the key. Ignoring the sweat gathering under my arms and on my forehead, I reread my perfectly rehearsed toast for the millionth time.

In an ill-conceived attempt to master my nerves, I was keeping the servers busy refilling my champagne glass. A little liquid courage never hurts, I thought.

Along with my top-notch champagne, I thoroughly enjoyed the creamy pasta and managed to forget that I am highly lactose intolerant. I had bigger concerns to worry about than my dietary issues. It wasn't until my stomach started gurgling that I became concerned.

Knowing that my big moment was coming up, I stepped away from the table and to a less crowded corner to let a silent one rip. Letting some of the pressure go was my only option, since I was next to speak.

In the worst possible cosmic timing, they announced my name, and everyone looked my way. I let loose a little control, and expecting a tiny puff, I was horrified at what happened next. Instead of a discreet release, I felt the worst possible betrayal; warm, immediate, and inescapable. Hot pudding started dripping down my leg, and the smell wafted from me.

My brain short-circuited. I smiled, and in a moment that I will never be able to forget, I reached for the closest appetizer tray and popped a stuffed jalapeno in my mouth. I clutched my throat, made eye contact with the nearest grandma, and mouthed the word "sorry" as if I was auditioning for community theater.

People closest to me were starting to make faces as the smell went rolling over them. I doubled down on my "choking" and scooted closer to the exit, my only hope and salvation. Everyone was staring at me and waiting for me to start my speech. Roughly 300 people dressed in their finest. I had to wave everyone off and make a run for it.

I hope my subterfuge managed to convince most of the room, but those people who were close enough to get a whiff knew full well what had happened. A quick stop at the lost and found dug up a pair of black jeans that were too short, but better poorly dressed than shit pants.

After getting cleaned up and disposing of the evidence (if not the smell in the bathroom), I carefully made my way back into the ballroom. After being reintroduced, I gave my epic speech, and to the applause, I bowed carefully, still not trusting my body not to betray me again. At no point did I make eye contact with the people sitting on the side that I had crop-dusted with my a** cologne.

We are still good friends to this day, and I think his wife is great. Maybe one day, after enough beer, I'll tell my buddy about my odd behavior, and that I hadn't almost choked at his wedding, but I haven't yet. They say college prepared us for the real world. But nothing could've prepared me for that toast.

FIRST DATE FIASCO

After months of no dating hell, I was finally excited about going out. I'd been set up with a great-looking guy that my friend had just bragged on. I'd been so busy at work that I was running on energy drinks and anxiety, but this promised to be a great diversion. Chugging one more energy drink, I squeezed into my hottest jeans and headed out.

We met at a casual restaurant that was quiet and perfect for getting to know each other on a first date. During the awkward small talk, I realized my stomach was starting to do strange things. When the apps were delivered, I held off eating anything, scared to add to the mounting pressure in my stomach, straining the waist of my jeans. Too bad my date insisted I try the cheese dip. As I leaned forward to scoop some up, gas started escaping, and I couldn't stop it. Panicked, I leaned back quickly only to squish.

Mortified, I sat really still, hoping to come up with a time machine to go back and get out of here. I know he heard it, and now he is making a face that tells me he has smelled it too. Everyone around us is waving their hands in front of their faces and looking around. I would have happily climbed under the table, but instead, I excused myself to the restroom.

I proceeded to penguin walk to the bathroom and get cleaned up as best I could. RIP my favorite underwear. Fifteen minutes and several texts from my date later, I reemerge and sit down. My date acted like nothing happened, and I apologized for taking so long. We've been married ten years now and have never spoken about that night again.

THAT TIME ON THE PLANE

I have one trip that I will never forget. It wasn't a trip I would ever repeat, but I'll never be able to wash it from my memory. I was on a flight that was oversold and stuck in the middle seat. Having never been in first class, I decided this was as good as it gets, and when you have to get from point A to point B, the middle seat is fine.

Of course, I was seated between a linebacker-sized guy hogging the armrest and a grandmother with a crochet project that kept poking me. With such a long flight in front of me, there was no relief in sight.

To make the trip all around more enjoyable, the couple behind me had a beautiful, bouncing boy about a year old. Little did I know that the squalling child behind me would be my saving grace.

Knowing I wouldn't be able to sleep under the circumstances, I had down multiple expressos before I boarded and asked for a coffee when the stewardess came by.

It turns out that enough caffeine turns your insides into a volcanic explosion. Thinking I might just be getting airsick, I asked for a ginger ale. Awful, awful plan. Several hours after leaving the Hartsfield-Jackson Atlanta International Airport, I was over nothing but water when my stomach started churning like the waves below.

Realizing that something horrible was about to happen, I attempted to crawl over the giant beside me. After making it over my friendly local boulder, I hustled to the bathroom to find it occupied. Discreetly weaving back and forth in an attempt to placate my gut, I felt small, soggy turds start to slip out.

There was no stopping the tide once it started, and I just had to stand there and keep a game face on until the bathroom finally opened, and I practically pushed the teenager out of the way to get in. There was no undoing the damage, so I just cleaned up as best I could and sent my shame to where all bathroom secrets go.

Arriving back in my seat, I sat down, thanking God I'd worn my trusty black yoga pants. My unofficial armor for bad decisions and long flights. Then the human mountain next to me suddenly sniffed and said, "I think that baby messed his breeches," and I nodded gamely. The old lady next to me turned around to ask the parents if he needed a diaper change, and I tried to appear interested.

Shocked, they apologized and said he had never made such awful smells. After checking his diaper, they continued to apologize for his gas. The next hour was spent discussing what they might have fed him. I think the final conclusion was the beets must have done it. Poor kid probably never got beets again because he was covering for me. No one ever realized.

Somewhere out there, there's a twenty-year-old man who still isn't allowed near beets. All because he unknowingly covered my worst mile-high betrayal.

GYM SHORTS
GONE WRONG

Here's the scene: I am not a "fitness girl." I own exactly two pairs of gym shorts, both from the clearance rack at TJ Maxx. I wear them when the laundry pile has reached unmanageable levels, and I do not have the emotional strength to reclaim my life. My hair was pulled back in a ponytail that screamed, "I tried, but I also didn't try that hard," and I was armed with a neon water bottle that made me look far more dedicated to my working out than I actually was. But it was New Year's, and one must attempt to follow resolutions!

Honestly, the plan was simple enough. Get on the treadmill, pretend to take the row machine for a spin, and sweat out at least twenty percent of the extra calories from the holidays. You know, just enough movement to earn a smoothie later. Well, the problem was, my stomach had other plans. Earlier that day, I'd grabbed one of those "super healthy" protein bars packed with strange fiber. Let me tell you: when the label says "cleansing," it's not lying. I didn't know how much I had to be "cleaned" out.

Halfway through my treadmill strut, I felt that unmistakable gurgle. I tried the usual mind tricks: It's just gas, you'll be fine, walk it off. Except, spoiler alert: I was not fine. The treadmill belt kept rolling, my stomach kept rebelling, and my body decided it was time for a very public betrayal.

It all went down so fast. One second, I was power-walking to Beyoncé, the next second, my so-called "moisture-wicking" shorts were wicking . . . in the absolute worst way possible. A hot, soggy betrayal spread through the fabric, and I froze like a deer caught in fluorescent gym lighting.

I grabbed my neon water bottle, as if hydration could save me, and made a break for it. Of course, nothing says "totally casual exit" like sprinting off a treadmill mid-song while clenching your cheeks. I thought I was subtle until I caught my reflection in the wall mirror— panicked face, ponytail swinging like a propeller, hot pink gym shorts with a new design.

The locker room was packed, naturally. Women adjusting sports bras, chatting about their macros, completely unaware that I had just reenacted a crime scene in polyester. I ducked into a stall, peeled off my shorts, and sacrificed them to the trash can like a soldier leaving the battlefield.

Did I go back out there? Absolutely not. I tied my oversized hoodie around my waist, slunk to my locker, and walked out like I had somewhere better to be. The smoothie shop never tasted so much like victory and shame blended with extra ice. That was my only foray into the gym.

THE ELEVATOR
OF SHAME

Only on Monday mornings do the elevators get so crowded. Everyone comes in at the last minute, trying to make the weekend last as long as possible. I am no exception, but looking back, that was the last Monday I herded in with the crowd.

I was holding my iced latte and critiquing my pencil skirt, shiny heels, and designer purse in the elevator door reflection. Glad I had my life together enough to look that hot, even if breakfast had been some leftover chili of questionable birthdate. A girl has got to have priorities, and breakfast food wasn't one of mine.

As I waltzed, and I do mean waltzed because I was looking amazing, my stomach suddenly started cramping. Sweat broke out on my hairline and I was holding onto the wall for dear life. The elevator was crammed with the HR manager, several people from my floor, IT guys, and my boss's secretary. Despite clenching every ass muscle I've ever had while walking in heels, a low, slow fart rolled out of me.

Just when I decided dying in shame wouldn't get me far enough away from the situation, a fluffy dookie decided it needed to come out too. That tight skirt and sexy panties weren't enough to hold it all in, and it plopped right behind my heels.

Ready to throw myself off the roof when I could make it up there, I felt myself turning bright red. It was my boss's secretary, a no-nonsense older woman who stopped on the next floor and invited everyone to get off. She had seen my shame on the floor and salvaged my pride by forcing everyone to exit.

They might know I tooted like a man living off beans, but the worst of it was hidden by her quick thinking and assistance in cleaning up. I went on to work at that company for five more years and just avoided anyone who had been on that elevator.

STAND-UP COMEDY
GONE TOO REAL

My job is to get up on stage and make people laugh. I make fun of myself all the time. That is what I am paid to do. But every comedian runs into something that is a little too embarrassing, and we won't talk about it on stage for all the money and glory in the world. My embarrassing moment just happened to me while I was on stage, so there was no saving me.

I was young, fresh to the stage, just setting up for a quick five-minute set at a local club. Never before had I suffered from stage fright, but this was my first break. My chance to make a name for myself. And I was nervous. Not, I'm going to meet my girlfriend's parents for the first time, nervous, but OMG, the cops have pulled me over, do I have a warrant out for my arrest, nervous.

I started strong, with some fun, relatable jokes that had the audience rolling. I was killing it. No doubt there was a Netflix special in my future. The second I started relaxing, all that pent-up anxiety burst out my a** in a stage shaking trumpet of sound. Everything went quiet. My fart had hit the microphone and thundered out of every speaker in the joint.

Thinking fast, I made a joke. "Well, we've all been here before, who hasn't farted on a stage in front of 200 people?" Silence. Dead silence. Apparently, no one else ever had. Trying to make it seem like I meant to do that, I decided to let another slip because it has to be funnier if I meant to do it, right? I leaned a little to the side, made a smooth one-liner, and let it rip.

So much more than I expected. Immediately, my pants sagged, and my heart stopped. I hadn't let out another unfunny fart. I'd just shat myself in front of 200 people who were already questioning my credentials. There is complete silence. Nothing but wide eyes staring back at me, waiting to see what my next move is. But I don't know what my next move is.

A guy in the front row whispers, "Did he just . . . ?" His wife whispers back, "Maybe it is part of the act?" Slowly, whispers break out across the full room. I wanted to leave an impression, not leave the stage with skid marks.

100

"Well, guys, that is how to make sure the audience is paying attention." I laugh awkwardly. A few brave audience members laughed brokenly along with me, but most of the crowd just stared. I start shuffling farther from the front of the stage, hoping the smell won't travel. "People always ask me why I wear black pants when I'm performing. Well, the best advice my mom ever gave me was to wear black in case of emergencies. This is probably not what she meant, but if it works, it works." More awkward laughing.

I pick back up my set, trying to get my jokes rolling again, when some a**hole on the front row suddenly yells, "It stinks." Quickly firing back I ask, "Me or my jokes?"

After several more painful moments, I wrap it up and let everyone know there is no need to applaud my rock bottom, but thank you, and they have been a great audience. At least everyone felt sorry enough to give me some applause. I haven't been back to that state since.

CAMPING MISHAPS & NATURE'S BETRAYAL

I figured a long weekend of roughing; it was just the vacation I needed. Me and some buddies grilling hotdogs over the fire and fishing for dinner. We thought we were so well-prepared: food, check; tent, check; fishing gear, check. It wasn't until we hiked fifteen miles to the campsite that we realized no one had brought toilet paper.

Not worried at all, we set up camp and started enjoying the great outdoors. It wasn't until day two that I started having a rumbling in my stomach that made me think eating ten hot dogs over two days might not have been the best choice.

We were out on the dock when I unexpectedly doubled over with violent stomach cramps and my stomach started releasing all ten hot dogs and everything else I had eaten in the last week. I waddled into the woods in search of a private tree to pop a squat, not even thinking about the lack of toilet paper. Twenty minutes later, my stomach finally decided that it had ejected enough hot lava.

Leaning against the rough bark, trying to catch my breath, I realized I was covered in sh*t and had no way to clean up. I grabbed some handfuls of leaves, but they all crumbled and left confetti spread across my butt cheeks. A couple of rocks were my next attempt and kindly exfoliated my a** for me. Pinecones — yeah, I moved on from that idea pretty quickly.

Snatching off my cleanest sock, I cleaned up as best I could. I buried my pants as a loss and made a streaker run to the pond yelling "cannonball" as I launched into the freezing cold water. The laughter from my buddies lasted until the next guy had to go. I wished him good luck, warned him to stay away from the poison ivy, and went back to fishing. The splash he made, having to jump in the lake next, was the best sound of the weekend.

THESE PEOPLE SURVIVED, SO CAN YOU

Hearing about other people's misfortunes can elicit empathy from you. Or sometimes it just makes you feel better because their story is WAY worse than yours.

As much as we want to feel sorry for other people, these stories are proof that you aren't out there alone. There is a whole club of people that have sharted themselves and survived. When the shart comes for you, just remember that other people have lived with the shame. They've gone on to have productive and fulfilling lives. No matter how awful you feel in the moment (whether embarrassment or stomach cramps), this is a moment that will pass. When you are ninety years old, you'll look back and be able to remember it without cringing.

[9]
THE SHART-PROOF LIFESTYLE

While you've learned a lot about how to shart-proof your life, I still have more to teach you, young grasshopper. So far, these helpful tips and facts have merely been the white-belt skills in the dojo of digestive disaster.

From home decor advice to some final dating knowledge, you aren't quite done with your master's in sharting.

DESIGNING YOUR HOME FOR FAST BATHROOM ACCESS

Let's start with your home's runway, the hallway. Make sure you keep the hallway clear of clutter at all times. There is nothing worse than taking off at a dead sprint, tripping over laundry baskets, empty Amazon boxes, and "I'll move that later" piles. Your hallway must be prepared for emergency runs.

If you have kids, make sure there is a bin at the end, out of the hallway, and make regular sweeps to get all the toys picked up. Legos are not the massage you want for your feet.

Keep your walkways open. Nobody wants to zig-zag through your ottomans and coffee tables when trying to move fast. Anywhere in your living room, you should have at least thirty inches of walkway space where nothing gets in the way.

That includes your favorite pretty chair and the floor lamp you just had to have. If you have to stop and step over anything in your living room, or dance around a table to avoid knocking over lamps, you have an overcrowded living room. Try cutting back. Nowhere in your home should it feel like a Mario Kart track.

Sharts don't just happen during the day. Nighttime sharting is a real possibility, also, so plan accordingly. You need lights to get from point A to point B, unless you are Catwoman. While leaving lights on at night and keeping your home illuminated in the wee hours will just leave your neighbors questioning your activities and criminal status, you do need to have some light options.

Make sure your overheads are working, so that when you reach a switch, you know it will come on. Also, place lamps throughout your home, like on your nightstand, to help you reach the light switches. If you find the option of having to hunt down lights and slow your race to the bathroom daunts you, there are other options.

Try installing motion sensor lights. Put one beside your bed, so when you hop out of bed, a light turns on. It doesn't have to be bright because you don't want to alert the household to your situation. Arrange the lights along the path to your powder room. That way, you can move fast and not stop for lights.

If you are in the enviable position of house hunting, keep in mind bathroom placement. A bathroom that is not connected to your bedroom is harder to get to. A bathroom that is one story and a couple of rooms away is a challenge. A bathroom that is two stories and several rooms away is a lost cause. You might as well pop a squat beside your bed and accept your fate.

Bonus points for anywhere that has multiple bathrooms. Even if the second or third bathroom is a half bath, it will still have a toilet, and that is the important part. You never know when a bathroom will be occupied, clogged, or under maintenance. Have a backup plan.

Make sure you have a conversation with your family. Everyone needs to have a clear understanding of the importance of leaving walkways clean, stairways free, and doorways unencumbered. You'll seriously consider getting rid of your kid if you trip over their latest favorite and poop yourself on the way down.

Also, clarify bathroom priorities. It's a toilet, not a library. Don't just hang out checking your phone, texting, scrolling, or reading. If you aren't doing serious business, get out and let the next person go.

THE CAR
SURVIVAL SETUP

Just like sharting isn't contained to daytime activities, it is not guaranteed to only happen at home. Another place that you might spend a lot of your time is in your car. It is best to be prepared there, as well.

Your car can be your rolling fortress, where even disasters can't take you down. No matter if you are stuck in a traffic jam, praying for the red light to change, or crossing your fingers in the drive-thru, make sure you are prepared. If you have ever been stuck in your car, you know that your colon has a sixth sense for picking the no-exit moments.

While every parent and car enthusiast knows the value of seat covers, it is time to take it to the next level. Car seat covers aren't just for stale cereal and muddy paw prints. In fact, their real value comes in the form of shart protection.

Vinyl or waterproof fabric will keep those butt surprises from leaking into your seats and the smell haunting you until you manage to sell the car to some poor fool. No amount of air freshener and denial will keep the scent from being your worst enemy. Imagine the dead of summer, with the heat that has baked every bad smell in the car, and it is just waiting on you to open the door and get nailed by the wave of putrid smell.

Keep several emergency towels in your car. That isn't just smart for your bowel disappointments, it is also just a good supply to have on hand. Having extra towels in your truck, along with a towel that's easily accessible at all times, is the best combination. You can use those towels if you leave the gym, need to wipe your windshield, or have a sudden nosebleed. Be like a Boy Scout: prepared for anything.

Stash just a few small trash bags in your glovebox. Make sure that the trash bags you choose are a dark color because white will only go so far when it comes to hiding your butt chocolate. Trash bags will help you get rid of evidence from your butt, your illegal crimes, and signs of your affair in emergencies.

Do a thorough search of your car when you first get it. Many cars come equipped with secret hideouts. Those hidey-holes might be the glove box, side door pockets, pockets on the back of seats, center console storage, or many other amazing places, as cars continue to evolve.

Just a good rule to remember when in the car is to avoid certain road trip staples. Gas station food, from sushi to chili to fried chicken, is usually a bad idea and should be avoided at all times. If the food has been prepared beside the beer and lotto tickets, your stomach might not appreciate the finer points of the culinary experience.

If you have a regular route that you travel for your commute, go ahead and be familiar with the best bathrooms. Running behind on your way to work and having to debate where to stop never ends well. Think of yourself as a NASCAR driver, and bathrooms as pit stops of survival.

THE BIDET-TO-GO: WHY IT'S THE REAL MVP

If you are trying to survive a shart attack, there is nothing better than having access to a bidet. While wipes and toilet paper will do the job, they aren't a cure-all, and sometimes you need something more effective. A nice reset on your heinie can make you feel better, instead of making you feel like you've just spread the problem around.

While you might understand the importance of a bidet, not every bathroom will have one, so it is best to ensure you have one at all times. The bidet-to-go is the MVP of the bathroom survival game.

A portable bidet can be manual or rechargeable. It is a water bottle with a superpower. The manual bidet is a squeezable bottle that works with an angled nozzle to reach all your crevices. Fill it with water (from the sink you heathen), aim (correctly, not at the ceiling), and squeeze. Amazingly effective, they are a simple tool to carry around, sometimes coming in collapsible versions.

The electric version does much of the same job, but you charge it up beforehand. It provides a steady stream of water that allows you to clean up quickly. They can hold enough water for several washes and have adjustable pressure settings. Some models can be used up to sixty-five times between charging, and that means you don't have to stress about charging it every night like your phone. Just put it on the charger once a week or so.

Oh, you might claim that you are fine using toilet paper, but what happens when it runs out? If there is no toilet paper to be found, you'll be wishing you had a travel bidet ready to go. Using water to rinse your tush also means that you won't have those little fuzzy paper balls stuck to any of your sensitive bits. Your butthole and other sensitive areas have already been through enough! Use water to keep that sensitive skin happy.

If you are concerned about people noticing that you are carrying around a butt washer, don't be. They are built with stealth in mind; most come with handy carrying cases or in a collapsible form. There is nothing better than having a surefire way to clean up after a stomachache when you are out living your best life globally or locally. If you are embarrassed to fill it up at the sink, just take a bottle of water with you. Don't let a twenty-dollar squeezable bottle be all that keeps you from reclaiming your dignity.

OTHER BATHROOM ACCESSORIES WORTH THE INVESTMENT

If you find that having a bidet is to your liking, and now, you want to know what else you can carry with you to enhance your bathroom experience, no worries. You can crap like a sultan with enough preparation, no matter what bathroom you are forced to endure. A peasant's bathroom doesn't mean you have to act like a peasant.

TRAVEL SHELF

Go ahead and shop around for a shelf that has suction cups on it. They are great in a bathroom that lacks comfort amenities. Perfect for placing bags and other accessories on, avoiding anything touching the nasty floor, where ghosts of sharts past live.

Test your shelf out at home and make sure that it holds well. Once you determine that it will hold, start checking the weight to see how much it will hold before it is overloaded and you have a wipeout. A durable and reliable shelf is the first step to making your toilet stall worthy of your superior rear.

TRAVEL CANDLE

There is no need to let the fluorescent lighting set the tone. Go ahead and bring a candle to set up on the back of the toilet, on the floor, or on your shelf. Double-check that your shelf is well-secured. There is nothing worse than it falling with your candle and setting your pants on fire. At least you wouldn't have to explain why they are stained anymore—they'll be burnt to a crisp.

Find nice, relaxing scents like lavender or eucalyptus so that you will have a spa-like experience, even if you are parking it at a truck stop. Not only will your candle help hide the smell of your activities, but it will also help make everyone else's bathroom experience better. Just remember your match or lighter.

PORTABLE BLUETOOTH SPEAKER

Once it smells nicer, there is no reason for you to have to listen to the symphony of bathroom noises. Hang, sit, or stand a Bluetooth speaker, and hook your phone up so that you can listen to your favorite tunes. Even if you don't want to listen to music, you can turn on nature sounds.

The speaker also covers up the sounds of your crisis so that no one has to know what you are up to. Or maybe you don't care that the entire bathroom knows what you are up to. Instead, you want to empower everyone to do their best business. Go ahead and create a soundtrack to encourage the bathroom at large and own what you are doing there. It might look like this:

- "Oops! ... I Did It Again" - Britney Spears
- "Let It Go" - Frozen Soundtrack
- "Who Let the Dogs Out" - Baha Men

- "Shake It Off" – Taylor Swift
- "Toxic" – Britney Spears
- "Sound of Silence" – Simon & Garfunkel
- "Wrecking Ball" – Miley Cyrus
- "Rolling in the Deep" – Adele
- "Hot in Here" – Nelly
- "Another One Bites the Dust" – Queen
- "Every Breath You Take" – The Police
- "Firework" – Katy Perry
- "Livin' on a Prayer" – Bon Jovi
- "Thunderstruck" – AC/DC
- "I Will Survive" – Gloria Gaynor
- "Highway to Hell" – AC/DC
- "All By Myself" – Celine Dion
- "Don't Stop Believin'" – Journey

YOUR STALL PLANT

There is no reason that a bathroom stall can't feel like a piece of home. Carry a small succulent with you to make the dreariest, saddest of commodes a little nicer. Succulents are portable and compact, allowing you to keep one in your bathroom bag while maintaining low maintenance. They don't need a lot of sun or water. So, you can focus on matters at hand and not watering your succulents during your bathroom time.

Live plants provide an air quality boost, which you might desperately need after being stuck in your stall for a while. Any little improvement in a stinky stall can help. If you decide that a live plant isn't what you need to keep with you, that's understandable. Try a fake succulent. There are many versions that look just like their live counterparts.

PORTABLE FANS

Ensure that you keep fresh batteries in a fan that you can hang or hold. The air in most bathrooms starts getting stale after sitting for a long time. Use the fan to help disperse the scent of your candle and keep the air fresh.

It can also get hot in a stall or public bathroom, so a small fan that keeps air on your face can be a lifesaver. Imagine sitting on the throne with your forehead dripping sweat, while your stomach cramps, trying to remove the offending materials from your insides. You slowly pass out from heat, exhaustion, and strain, leaving the local fire department to use the jaws of life to extract you. Or you have a nice fan that keeps you cool and calm.

HEATED TOILET SEAT

If you have ever sat down on a cold toilet, you'll know it is an unpleasant feeling. There is no need to suffer through hypothermia on your bum when you can bring your very own soft and heated toilet seat.

A plush seat will keep blood circulating and your toes from going to sleep. Add in a healthy dose of heat to smooth those sore buttock muscles, and you won't have to be in a hurry to hop up and rejoin the party because you'll be having your very own party in the loo.

DATING WHILE SHARTING

You already know to be aware of your clothing choices. You don't necessarily need to wear black. Throw on a flowy patterned skirt or some brown pants if you are concerned — anything to camouflage the brown stain of shame.

It is common sense to control the transportation situation. If you are stuck in their car, there is no escape, and you'll probably have to pay to get their car detailed if you have a runny oops. Drive yourself or arrange your own way to stay out of that situation.

When you are saying hello, be careful of the hug. Clenching for dear life, trying to keep your lunch inside, is an awful place to be when someone comes in for a hug. That squeeze might be the tipping point of pressure to let it all go. Aim for a side hug instead.

But what do you do when the worst happens, and you aren't sure how to explain the smell, the sound, or the sudden need for a bathroom dash? There are some great options that will keep your date moving or at least make it the most memorable date they've ever had.

DATING SHART EXCUSE ONE:

Go ahead and own up. You both know something unfortunate happened—there is no hiding it at your two-foot intimate table. Try some lines like, "Well, that's not usually my first move. Excuse me while I go reset." "That's not the impression I was planning on leaving, but give me just a few moments and I'll try again." Or "Hey, I don't believe in hiding who I really am— now you get to see the real me." Whether you go back to the table after getting cleaned up is up to you.

If all else fails, when your stomach rumbles, lean forward and whisper with a serious face, "That was my spirit animal."

DATING SHART EXCUSE TWO:

If you have a little space and might pull off the "what's that smell" option, there are several factors you can blame your odor on: "Wow, they really need to do something about the plumbing in here!" "That squirrel seems to have let one rip." Or "Someone definitely smuggled a whoopee cushion into this establishment."

As a last-ditch resort, try to convince them of something they might have seen on TV: "I think Ghost Hunters did an episode here because they have flatulent ghosts."

DATING SHART EXCUSE THREE:

This could be the perfect time to see if your date is competitive or has a sense of humor. The couple that can fart and shart together is the couple that stays together. When you let a juicy one go, ask something like, "Your move. Can you top that one?" "I find dates are better with soundtracks—let's hear yours." Or "What would I score if this were an Olympic event?"

To truly shift the limelight to them, challenge them with, "That was the opening act—let me hear your main event."

DATING SHART EXCUSE FOUR:

Go ahead and turn the moment into a grand, romantic gesture. It might not be the romance they were dreaming of, but some romance is better than none: "If we can survive this on a first date, we'll survive anything together." "The next thing I give you to smell will be roses." Or "They say love stinks—we must be in love."

Many people love rom-coms, so try to spin it as one: "Not what I planned, but some of my favorite rom-coms had this same plot."

LIFESTYLE READINESS CHECKLIST: ARE YOU SHART-PROOF?

Score yourself by checking each box that applies. Tally your points at the end to see how shart-proof your lifestyle really is.

HOME SETUP

- My hallway and living room have clear "runways" for bathroom sprints, nothing to trip over.
- I have a motion-sensor or night lights for safe midnight dashes, avoiding injuries.
- Everyone in my household knows the "bathroom priority" rule, and we have talked about it.
- I have at least two bathrooms or access to a backup plan.

CAR SURVIVAL

- My car has waterproof seat covers, and I keep them on there.
- I keep dark trash bags stashed in the glovebox, along with gloves.
- Emergency towels are stored in an easy-to-grab spot but tucked out of sight.
- I know at least three reliable bathroom stops along my usual route.

BATHROOM ACCESSORIES

- I own a portable bidet and am comfortable using it.
- I have all my luxury bathroom items packed to carry with me at all times.
- I carry a small emergency kit (wipes, spare underwear, deodorizer, all the good stuff).

DATING SURVIVAL

- I've got a foolproof clothing plan, incorporating black pants, a flowy skirt, or a camo pattern.
- I have at least one excuse/joke ready for a bathroom emergency to try and smooth things over.

○ I drive myself on dates or make sure I control my own ride.

[10]
TRAVEL INSURANCE: GLOBE-TROTTING WHILE SHARTING

When you're ready to start your world tour, be aware that not all countries have equal bathroom facilities. Real travel insurance involves planning the countries you are going to visit based on their bathroom situation. Take a look at some of the bathrooms you might encounter.

JAPAN

Known for their advanced technology options, their bathrooms are no exception. バスルーム or Basurūmu, is a Japanese bathroom that often has a washlet-style electronic bidet. These toilets have mind-blowing features like heated seats, warm-water sprays for cleaning, air dryers, and deodorizers. You might even get lucky and discover a toilet with ambient music, called the Sound Princess or Otohime, which helps disguise the sound of nature taking its course.

To make using the bathroom extra fun, the toilet seat might be motion-activated, or the toilet might be equipped with a control panel. Good luck figuring out which one will get your bum clean and which one will give you a colon cleanse. It isn't quite like driving a spaceship, but it might be as close as you ever get.

There are Shigeru Ban stalls in Shibuya, Tokyo, that have clear stall walls, but don't think everyone wants to watch you do your business. When you look at the door, the stalls become opaque.

If you are visiting a local, be sure to look for the "toilet slippers" when you go to the bathroom. They are only to be worn inside the bathroom. It will greatly offend your host if you wear them out of the bathroom. The Japanese take their bathrooms so seriously that there is an entire museum, the TOTO Museum in Kitakyushu, that is dedicated to the history of Japanese toilets.

INDIA

While you might be used to sitting on your toilet, that is not the case in all countries. In India, there are traditional toilets called squat toilets. They are holes in the ground with footrests so that you can squat instead of sitting. Because of tradition, affordability, and hygiene, squatting toilets can still be found in many parts of India. Because the butt never makes contact with a seat, they are thought of as cleaner than Western options.

Not all their toilets are squat toilets, and Western potties are also available. But toilets haven't been as common in India as in some countries. In 2014, Swachh Bharat Mission (Clean India Mission) was launched, with the goal of eradicating open pooping and encouraging toilet use. In the following five years, ninety million households had toilets installed.

No matter what kind of toilet you manage to find in India, don't be surprised if you can't find toilet paper. The bucket and cup method is much more popular. Called lota, the water is used to clean after going to the bathroom. If you have sharted, it could be a beneficial option. It is much easier to clean up when you have a bucket of water.

Japan is not the only country that takes their bathrooms seriously. In Delhi, the Sulabh International Museum of Toilets that gives visitors a history of sanitation dating back to 3000 BC.

CHINA

Another country that is well known for its use of squat potties is China. If you are on the hunt for one because you want a new bathroom experience, make sure to look in rural areas, where they will be the most commonly used option.

In major Chinese cities, public restrooms are often clean, staffed, and free of charge. Make sure you consider where you are bathroom hunting because once you are away from urban areas, it might be a good idea to carry your own soap and toilet paper.

Nothing worse than finally finding a bathroom and not having toilet paper, but rural public spaces are not always equipped for visitors. Once you have used the toilet paper, whether personal or provided, look to see if there is a bin to dispose of it. A lot of bathrooms can't handle flushed toilet paper.

China takes its bathroom seriously. They boast the Porcelain Palace, which is over 32,200 square feet in size and is dedicated to the bathroom arts. It has more than 1,000 stalls, making it the largest in the world. Located in Chongqing and featuring Egyptian-inspired architecture, it is a must-see for any bathroom enthusiast. The place has some of the world's most unique commodes; think open crocodile mouth toilets or the Virgin Mary gracing the top of the tank. And I bet you thought your porcelain throne at home was nice.

MIDDLE EAST

While it is not uncommon to find squat toilets or Western toilets in the Middle East, there is one aspect that might confuse you once you perch atop a Middle Eastern commode.

The Shattaf, also known as a bum gun, health faucet, or bidet shower, is the preferred method for cleaning up for most people. It is a small, handheld nozzle that connects to the water supply. It is supposed to do the job of toilet paper by making you clean. With it, you are one small button away from a clean bum.

Using the sprayer instead of toilet paper reflects the Islamic hygiene practices that demand washing after relieving. Using the water is a sign of purity and fits with the cultural norms in the area. Some bathrooms will have toilet paper, but it is expected to only be used for drying.

While visiting the Middle East, know that you aren't supposed to wipe your butt with your right hand or shake hands. The left hand is for eating and touching other people, while the right is reserved for self-cleaning.

MEXICO

A lot of the toilets you run across in Mexico might have a manual flushing system. If the handle doesn't work or there isn't one, look for a bucket nearby. A bucket, or cubo, is kept filled with water. The water in the bucket replaces the tank system you might be used to. Just pour the water in the toilet, and it will wash your waste away.

Mexico is another country where you might find a waste basket for toilet paper nearby. Always inquire before using someone's restroom if you aren't sure. The last thing you want to be remembered as is the tourist who flooded their bathroom.

Not all toilets are created equal in Mexico. If you encounter a toilet without a seat, it was probably meant to be that way to save money or to make cleaning easier. Don't worry, there isn't a toilet seat bandit roaming the countryside.

While bathrooms in Mexico might be missing running water, a toilet seat, and paper, they are some of the most beautiful bathrooms you might have the privilege of using. Some of the bathrooms showcase Talavera porcelain toilets in bright colors and intricate designs. The tile in the rooms can also look more like art than a place to do your smelly business. At least you'll have a view while you clean yourself up after too many tacos and an embarrassing shart.

AUSTRALIA

If you have never been, Australia is not known as the land of water. In 1980, an Australian named Bruce Thompson came up with a way to conserve water. The dual flush toilet doesn't have the traditional wiggle handle on the front; instead, it has two buttons on top of the tank.

The smaller button is used for liquid waste, dispensing just three liters of water, while the larger button takes care of more solid matters, with six liters to wash it away. Amazingly, the system saves sixty-seven percent of water compared to a traditional Western toilet.

So don't be alarmed if you see this double feature. Either button will take care of most waste, but use the larger one if you are dealing with a blowout. The good news is that every bathroom should come with toilet paper, so you don't have to navigate any new butt cleaning techniques, and you'll be able to easily find a bathroom.

GERMANY

Known as a Flachspüler, the flat flusher toilet is built differently. There is a porcelain shelf where your poop lands instead of in water. The poop will sit there until flushed. While becoming less popular, this design was to conserve water and reduce splashing. We've all had the sudden splash back that comes with big poops, and it isn't a pleasant experience. Maybe they are on to something.

The shelf also allows for your stool to be looked at for health reasons. A lot of common health problems can be diagnosed by looking at your stool. Practically speaking, cleaning up after your poop has sat on a shelf is necessary, so there should be a toilet brush nearby to handle the remains after flushing.

The shelves tend to get stained, so be sure to clean as soon as possible, and be glad you are not the person in charge of scrubbing the sh*t shelf. If you are having an unpleasant moment, the smells can also be overwhelming because your excrement is not in water, and the smell is free to wander.

Don't be surprised if, while you are traveling the Autobahn, a network of federal highways with no speed limit, you run across bathrooms that aren't free to use. Most service stations require you to pay for the use of their facilities, and they might not accept electronic payment. Keep coins on hand in case of a bathroom emergency so you can use the toilet.

BUSES, TRAINS, & PLANES, OH MY

Buses are not known for their luxury travel. Even the high-end tour buses can only take comfort so far. Bathrooms are tucked into the back corner of buses, and you have to walk by everyone between you and the back to get to the bathroom. If you have to handle some serious business, people are sitting just a couple of feet away while you do it.

Don't forget, not all roads are created equally. While you are in the bathroom trying to clean up or use the facilities, you can expect bumps, stops, turns, and, if you are truly unlucky, a rear-end collision. Just know that whatever necessities you have to take care of in the bathroom need to be done as quickly as possible.

From the time you have an unfortunate shart on the bus, leaving dingy stains on the seat, to the time you try to air out in the tiny stall, allowing the smell to waft throughout the bus, you are public enemy number one.

While more forgiving than a bus, a train still isn't the most ideal spot to have a shart catastrophe. Usually more luxurious than a bus bathroom, trains also tend to have a smoother ride and less foot traffic. Some trains will have multiple bathroom areas, which allows the crowds to spread out. If you're lucky and find a newer train, you can even find a bathroom with all the amenities of a land bathroom, like a mirror, vanities, and even changing tables (make sure to strap in your baby—you are still moving).

Like many bathrooms, sometimes you run across broken bathroom locks. There is nothing worse than having your pants around your ankles and toilet paper wrapped around both hands, trying to clean up when the door suddenly swings open.

While using a train bathroom, make sure to take advantage of those horns to really relieve some pressure.

Stumbling into an airplane bathroom that looks straight out of a space station means that you have landed yourself in the Mile-High Club. Well, the Shart Mile-High Club. The good news is that airplane bathrooms work. They'll dispose of your evidence well.

Contrary to the sound that little toilet makes when it opens up, you aren't dropping your waste onto unsuspecting people on the ground. That shameful evidence is vacuum sucked away, and it all goes to a special compartment. Airplanes are so loud that most sounds you make will be covered up by the engines. So, you'll be able to finish your business quickly.

While you have plenty of options for your shart events while travelling, none of them are ideal. Just do the best you can, and respect the bathroom of whatever country you are in. Customs are a vital part of enjoying your travel experience.

QUICK COMPARISON FOR TRAVELERS

MIDDLE EAST:

- Western toilet and shattaf sprayer
- Water-based hygiene standard
- Toilet paper often for drying only

INDIA

- Squat toilets or bucket and lota setups
- Jug of water for cleaning

- Toilet paper uncommon

CHINA

- Mostly squat toilets; some Western
- Carry your own paper & soap
- Toilet paper often goes in the bin, not flushed

JAPAN

- High-tech washlet bidet toilets
- Heated seats, spray options, music, and motion sensors

MEXICO

- Western toilets; bucket & cubo for flush
- Toilet paper often goes in the bin
- Talavera porcelain designs in some bathrooms

AUSTRALIA

- Dual-flush Western toilets
- Two-button system saves water
- Widely available toilet paper

GERMANY

- Flat-flusher (Flachspüler) toilets
- Poop lands on the shelf for inspection
- Toilet brush always nearby

SOME FINAL PARTING THOUGHTS

You should be wiser after reading this. After crawling through the trenches of shart survival, you should be proud of yourself, and more prepared than most people will ever manage to be. You might also have unlocked some new fears, but that is part of the maturing and learning process.

You know the warning signs. You have a better understanding of your gut. You have emergency kits stashed in several locations. You keep a mental map of exit strategies. You rank bathrooms in your free time. You are now a Shart Master.

As prepared as you are, life will still catch you unsuspecting and knock you out with a curveball. Your body will betray you on the worst possible day, in front of the worst possible people, but at least you'll be able to think through the panic. You'll survive, along with the other thirty-three percent of the world.

While it might seem like the worst moment of your life, it is just a moment. In a life full of amazing moments, don't let this be the one that holds you back. Know that this pants-ruining, dignity-destroying, and story-creating moment will be a moment to look back on, and as long as you use the knowledge you learned here, you'll be okay.

The goal in writing this book wasn't to make you shart-proof; nothing can do that. The goal in writing this book was to make you shart-prepared, shart-confident, and shart-shameless. Knowing more about how your body functions and what can cause sharts should make you more forgiving of yourself and your butt.

Your worth as a human being has nothing to do with your bowel control. Everyone will have weak moments. It doesn't make you a gross person or a broken one. It just means your human body is going through something. Listen to your body.

Society is what has taught you shame. It is a learned feeling, and you should relearn that natural body functions aren't failures. Just an inconvenience.

MEDICAL DISCLAIMER

While sharting can be a hilarious life event, it can also indicate a serious health problem. If you experience incontinence, regularly consult your medical provider. Symptoms like blood in stool, severe pain, and frequent accidents should be reported immediately. Also, contact your doctor if you have bowel movements that are out of the normal color range. Nothing in this book should be taken as medical advice and should only be used for entertainment.

www.ingramcontent.com/pod-product-compliance
Lightning Source LLC
Chambersburg PA
CBHW061649120626
46550CB00003B/884